Stepping Out on Faith

Saying Goodbye to Public Education after 19 Years

Dr. Marilyn S. Mitchell-McCluskey

Copyright © April 2018 Dr. Marilyn Mitchell-McCluskey

All rights reserved. No part of this publication may be reproduced, distributed or transmitted in any form or by any means, including photocopying, recording, or other electronic or mechanical methods, without the prior written permission of the publisher, except in the case of brief quotations embodied in critical reviews and certain other noncommercial uses permitted by copyright law. For permission requests, write to the publisher, McCluskey & Associates, LLC, P.O. 1605, Cedartown, Georgia 30125 or email authormarilynmccluskey@gmail.com.

I have tried to recreate events, locales, and conversations from my memories and correspondences to include emails, social media and text messages. In some instances, I have changed the names of individuals who I do not respect enough to have their names appear in **my** book. Others I changed to protect their anonymity.

Stepping Out on Faith:
Saying Goodbye to Public Education after 19 Years
ISBN-10: 1985697378
ISBN-13: 978-1985697379

DEDICATION

This book is dedicated to Mrs. Gracie Jefferson, Mr. Ronald Peterson, Mr. George Folsom, Mrs. Carolyn Kerr Hamilton, Dr. Gail Fowler, Dr. Missoura Ashe, Dr. Edward Wilson, Mr. Keith Hose, Mrs. Ishia Dawson, Mrs. Tina McBride, and Dr. Clifton Nicholson...former administrators who touched my life along my journey in education.

A special dedication to my guardian angel, Dr. Sherrell Newton. Not a day goes by that I don't think of you. I finally finished a book as I promised.

CONTENTS

INTRODUCTION 9
1 TROUBLEMAKER 14
2 EDUCATION UP NORTH 40
3 BACK IN GEORGIA 53
4 POMP AND CIRCUMSTANCES 77
5 MOVE ON WHEN READY 88
6 SAT VERSUS ACT 102
7 COLLEGE NIGHTS 114
8 DR. MCCLUSKEY CARES 127
9 INDEBTED TO ME 135
10 THE WOLVES' DEN 146
11 WHEN IN ROME 156
12 THE DIGITAL LEARNING LAB 175
13 ON A MISSION 190
14 FROM EIGHTY-SIX TO ZERO 199
15 KNOW YOUR RIGHTS 205
16 UP, UP, AND AWAY! 216
17 TIME FOR A CHANGE 221
18 THE NEW PRINCIPAL 231
19 THE FIRST MONTH 237

20 RESIGNATION 252

21 THE WORLD'S GREATEST PARENTS 270

22 OUTCAST 278

23 STEPPING OUT ON FAITH 294

EPILOGUE 304

ACKNOWLEDGEMENTS

I would first like to acknowledge my husband, Derrick William McCluskey, Sr. Throughout all of my trials and tribulations, this man has been my rock, sword, and shield.

Secondly, I would also like to acknowledge my children, Marion, McKenzie, Blanche, and Derrick, Jr. Thanks for allowing mommy to write her first book.

To my parents, Thomas and Linda Gosier, and Marion and Velvie Mitchell, thanks for pushing me to be great; and to my siblings: Marion, Angela, Thomas, Glen, Johnny, Allison, and Anthony…many thanks for your unwavering support and continuous motivation.

I would also like to acknowledge my grandparents, Ulysses, Sr. and Johnnie Marable and the entire Marable clan. We are still putting Dixie on the map.

To my good friend, Shannon Roper, you can finally get some sleep now. Thank you so much for listening to me read countless pages and providing much needed feedback.

Without hesitation, I would like to acknowledge my friend and fellow author, Vernard "Julio" Hodges. You wrote Bet on Yourself: from Zero to Millions to provide the blueprint for financial success and then encouraged me to share my story and create a blueprint for success in education. I am forever grateful for your guidance and unwavering support through my writing process.

Lastly, I would like to acknowledge my publishing dream team: my editor, Ms. Barbara Joe, cover designer, Melinda Michelle, and proof readers, Kiera J. Northington, Chantel Marable-Moore, Dr. Dawnyetta Marable, Moriah Banks and Shannon Roper. Thank you for encouraging me to keep going!

INTRODUCTION

If you were to ask someone what they thought the most honorable professions were, teaching would probably rank pretty high on the list. That's because educators are held in high regards on account of the influential roles they represent in the lives of developing youth and advancement of the communities where they live and work.

That sounds great in theory!

Please don't be disappointed at the acknowledgment that all educators are not created equally nor are they all working for the betterment of our children. There are far too many who have infiltrated the career that I love passionately who only desire the summers off and a monthly paycheck.

There are two major factors that influenced me to become a teacher: a legacy of education and my desire to touch the lives of others.

At the age of five, I can vividly remember informing my kindergarten teacher and classmates that I would be attending Fort Valley State College in Fort Valley, Georgia where I would be living in Davison Hall, the dorm across from the cafeteria; pledging "pink and green" like my aunts (I instead chose to pledge blue and white like my uncles, brother, cousins and my hubby); and majoring in Animal Science so I could become a dentist like my two uncles had planned.

These were major dreams for a little scrawny kid from Dixie, Georgia, attending a small elementary school that housed grades K-7; however, my dreams were not uncommon in my family.

My grandfather would have it no other way!

He ALWAYS stressed the importance of receiving an education. This "legacy of education" was instilled in all ten of his children, his grandchildren, and everyone in our community that was fortunate to interact with him. According to my grandfather, there were NO EXCUSES for not receiving an education.

As he constantly explained to me during my childhood (and I constantly explain to the students that I teach), "You don't have to walk miles anymore, because there are now buses to transport you to and from school; you don't have to eat mayonnaise sandwiches like I did, because the school has a cafeteria that provides hot nutritious lunches; you don't have to sit in uncomfortable classrooms, because your school building is equipped with central air and heat; and you don't have to worry about not having worn, outdated books, because your school has brand new books and plenty of resources; you simply don't have any excuses not to get your education."

I could have entered the field of medicine and/or dentistry like the majority of my family and reaped the financial rewards that the profession provides, but anybody who knows me will quickly attest to the fact that I genuinely love to help others, especially students. My desire to touch the lives of others oftentimes drives my husband crazy. Frequently, he will ask, "Is anyone else doing this?" According to him, it appears I am often doing more than is required. *His pet name for me is Ghetto Oprah!* He swears that I have Oprah's giving spirit, just not her money. For years, my husband, like many others, failed to understand that if I can make the difference in one student's life, that student may go forward and make the difference in someone else's life, just because of my actions. I don't mind going above and beyond if it will make a difference. My husband is now my biggest source of encouragement and most gracious benefactor.

My greatest contribution to education is being able to share my grandfather's legacy. Like my grandfather, I impart the importance of receiving a quality education with not only my students, but with everyone I encounter. As George Washington Carver once stated, "Education is the key to unlock the golden door of freedom." There are so many people that are shackled in life because they did not adequately prepare themselves. Unfortunately, many fail to realize that it is never too late to get an education. In my adult education classes, we often discussed lifelong learning, and it is this phenomenon that I posit to my students, their parents, my co-workers, and friends. I encourage them to never stop learning, never give up, and never make excuses. Another favorite saying of mine is the Chinese Proverb: Give a man a fish and you feed him for a day. Teach a man to fish and you feed him for a lifetime. My students are encouraged to take charge of their education. I implore them to not passively wait to be given fish, but instead actively fish for themselves. I tell them, "Don't wait for someone to teach you, YOU are the greatest teacher in your life."

Many people may think that my greatest accomplishment in education is the obtainment of my doctorate from The University of Georgia; however, I beg to differ. Although, I am extremely proud of that feat, I feel my greatest educational accomplishments occur each time one of my students becomes a productive member of society. Their success, whether earning a college degree, entering the military, or gaining reputable employment, makes me feel proud to be a teacher, because I know that I played a role in their development.

I guess you are wondering why in the world do I want to walk away from a profession it is evident that I love. The hardships and betrayals that most people probably think are nonexistent in education have taken their toll on me. I will never walk away from educating children; I am simply walking away from public education as it is today.

I wrote this book to expose the detriment that has resulted in ineffective teaching, uneducated children, and poorly performing schools. I hope my journey will inspire you to be courageous enough to analyze your child's learning environment and employ the power you possess as parents, guardians, and stakeholders to make a difference. I am happy to be able to impart to you the knowledge it took me 19 years to learn. Hopefully this information can enable you to become an integral part of your child's education.

What has been done for so long in the dark, I now get to bring to the light – as I step out on faith.

1 TROUBLEMAKER

My so-called troublemaking did not begin until around my seventh year of working in education. I had witnessed many injustices during those years. Like most teachers across this nation, I kept my mouth firmly closed. It hurt like hell to remain quiet, but I had a house and car to pay for each month. It hadn't taken me long to realize that those who spoke up often found themselves out of a job.

It wasn't until after I got married in 2002 that I became bolder. It's true what they say about two incomes being better than one. After I became Mrs. Derrick McCluskey, I knew if I lost my job for being vocal about an issue, my hubby would be able to support me until I found another one. Ironically, I never looked for battles to fight; for some unknown reason, they always landed in my lap.

My first battle took place in Lake City, Florida. I left my job in Macon, Georgia, to accompany my husband, who was stationed at the National Guard Armory there. Leaving Southwest High School was bittersweet because Dr. Gail Morris Fowler was a phenomenal administrator. During the three years that I taught there, I learned a lot about the world of education. She was one of a few administrators who embraced my creativity and used my impulsiveness to her advantage. Dr. Fowler was extremely supportive, which made me work super hard for her. Although I didn't have a clue about cheerleading, I became her cheerleading coach for a year after she asked me to take on the task. Thankfully, one of the girl's parents, Ms. Valerie Hand, was my savior. I guess you could say I was her assistant coach.

I also supervised the yearbook, which had not been published for a couple of years, and continued to supervise my students from Florida to make sure our third book was completed. When I left Southwest, Dr. Fowler became a mentor and friend.

While teaching in Lake City, I was given a schedule that included regular and advanced classes. This was my first experience with middle school classes being leveled. I had taught middle school science and math during my first two years of teaching before I transitioned to high school and neither of those schools had leveled classes; thus, this concept was interesting to me. It wasn't until classes began that I considered the true purpose of these leveled classes was to segregate students.

My regular classes were filled with mostly children of color, and my advanced class was practically all white. There were two black kids, and one of them appeared to be mixed. Although the segregation was somewhat upsetting, what upset me most was the class size. Whereas my regular classes were maxed out with 25 or more students, the advanced class didn't have more than twelve students. It was then I noticed that all of the advanced classes the school offered had extremely low numbers, which didn't make any sense. Being that I was new to town, I didn't desire to make any waves, so I settled in and taught my social studies class without incident.

The trouble didn't begin until I requested a black female, Felicia, be moved from my regular class to my advanced class. Our counselor, Della, was adamant this move would not occur. According to her, Felicia needed certain grades. She had earned them. It was apparent Felicia was extremely intelligent. Her intelligence is why I wanted her moved to my advanced class. Though her behavior was sometimes subpar, I was confident moving Felicia would even improve that because she would finally be challenged. Then Della said her mother had to approve the move. Initially, Felicia's mother was hesitant because Della had frightened her somewhat by telling her that the advanced coursework was so much harder than the coursework in the regular class. I assured the mother that Felicia would be fine, and she signed the paperwork.

Still no move.

Della was dead set against moving Felicia into the advanced class. She had the principal call me in to inform me that Felicia would not be moving.

I asked, "Why?"

I will never forget as long as I live what Della responded. She looked me in my face and said, "I don't want to mix those going to Yale with those going to jail!"

That's when trouble found me.

I informed the principal and Della that Felicia would be moving because all of the criteria had been met, and I was going to pursue this issue with the superintendent and board of education if I needed to.

After calling the board's office to set up an appointment with the superintendent, I was given an appointment with the assistant superintendent, Mr. Bradley. Imagine my surprise to discover that the assistant superintendent was a black guy. I explained everything that had occurred, and he agreed there was no reason Felicia could not be moved to my advanced class. Mr. Bradley approved the move, which my principal never objected in the first place. Mr. Bradley also requested a listing of all classes and acknowledged I was correct that most of the advanced classes had very few students, some as little as seven students. I don't think the principal was even aware of the discrepancies in class sizes. He was a nice guy, but it was no secret, he was biding his time until his retirement, which was around the corner.

Della quit midyear, and I was happy she did. It was clear she held stereotypical views that were causing more harm than good. I taught for another year in Lake City before it was time to move again

RICHMOND COUNTY

My husband's next duty station was Fort Gordon, Georgia, located in Richmond County. We moved there the summer of 2004. I had given birth to our daughter, McKenzie, in January and was contemplating becoming a stay-at-home mom for a year. I didn't make it through the summer. I missed teaching. Luckily, getting a job in Augusta was not difficult at all, and I looked forward to teaching sixth-grade math.

This time, my principal, Donald, was a young black guy. He seemed to be pretty cool. For a while, things were sailing along smoothly until trouble fell in my lap again.

Donald and the bus drivers were at war because the buses were frequently late. Unfortunately, my students were caught in the middle. Those who arrived on a late bus were told to report directly to class, and not eat any breakfast. I didn't realize this had been going on for a couple of weeks until the students finally complained to me. Not wanting to cause any trouble, I went to Sam's Club and purchased breakfast bars for the late students to eat when they arrived. This worked well for a couple of weeks until my husband discovered what I was doing.

Considering my husband comes from humble beginnings himself, he became upset. He was well aware of the fact that for many kids, the school meals may be the only meals they get each day.

"You need to talk to your principal," he encouraged me.

I talked to Donald, and he refused to budge.

Next, I called the director of nutrition at the central office and asked if she was aware of the fact my students were being denied breakfast. She was appalled and informed me the students could not be denied breakfast, especially if their buses were late due to no fault of their own.

I guess she called Donald's boss, as it soon became apparent, he was livid with me. From that point on, my students were allowed to eat breakfast, but I now had a bull's eye in the center of my chest.

I eventually ended up in the assistant superintendent's office. Donald had become irate after I informed him that I would be recording a conversation that he and I were about to have. He was adamant that I not record him. I was adamant I would not be talking to him without recording him because he lied too much. Ever since I had called the nutrition's office on him, Donald had been tyrannical toward me.

The situation could have been far worse if I had not become friends with one of the teachers, Michelle "JW" Johnson-Wilson, who was a local. She is still a very good friend of mine. I guess you could say, JW was the mediator between *the Donald* and myself.

When I arrived at the assistant superintendent's office, Donald made sure he told his boss, Dr. Missoura Ashe, that I liked to record conversations.

Dr. Ashe asked me, "Are you recording now?"

I replied, "I only record people who I don't trust, and you have not given me a reason not to trust you."

Donald had the audacity to tell her to check my bag. My recorder was in my bag, but it was off. I gladly offered my bag to her, and to my surprise, she peeped inside and examined my recorder.

It was off.

I don't specifically remember our entire conversation, but I undoubtedly remember Donald whining to Dr. Ashe, "She doesn't act like this at school. Don't let her fool you."

I replied, "And he doesn't either. Don't let him fool you!"

Dr. Ashe appeared to be amused and dismissed us without any disciplinary action being taken against me. I stuck around for a few minutes after Donald left; I wanted to share with Dr. Ashe that she and I were both members of the same sorority, Zeta Phi Beta Sorority, Incorporated. I had noticed our paraphernalia in her office.

Although she has never specifically told me, I think Dr. Ashe knew I was being retaliated against by Donald because of my reporting him to the nutrition director.

When I returned to her office a couple of weeks later to ask for a transfer, she allowed me to move to the middle school with no hesitations.

I will forever be grateful to Dr. Ashe for making sure the remainder of my tenure in Richmond County was a good one.

POLK COUNTY

It's 2018, and I am still upset with my husband for not warning me about his hometown, Cedartown, Georgia. Moving to Cedartown in 2006 was like going through a time warp. Unbelievably, I met people who still used the word "colored."

My husband didn't see anything wrong with his hometown because he was born and raised there. From birth, he had been taught his place and didn't even realize that he stayed in it. I, on the other hand, was born and raised in South Georgia and matriculated through schools that had diverse teachers. To make a long story short, I was not prepared to be the only black teacher at Cedartown Middle School (CMS).

The student population was almost evenly divided by Blacks, Hispanics, and Whites; yet, all of the teachers were white. Many of the students had never had a black teacher before, so they didn't know what to expect from me. Although the teachers complained about students' behaviors, I told them their students behaved well compared to some of the places I had been.

Having only one chocolate chip in a cookie is not

satisfying and being the only black teacher in an entire school was not either. Thank God, my room was next door to Mrs. Debbie Alford and across the hall from Mrs. Kena Womack. These two teachers were lifesavers for me that year.

My assistant principal, Leanne, didn't particularly care for me from day one. Many black women in Cedartown were maids or housekeepers, including my husband's grandmother, and I think Leanne saw me in that light. She disrupted my class and didn't even acknowledge me. We eventually ended up getting into a confrontation after she had once again spoken to me in a demeaning manner.

I informed Leanne that I was not her slave nor her maid, and she would never talk to me in said manner again, particularly in front of my students.

She reported me to the principal who, in turn, informed me that Leanne was my boss, and I had better do what she said. I let both of them know that neither of them signed my check and I respected authority but certainly didn't fear it. At that point, I knew the year was going to be a horrible one, and I started planning an exit strategy.

The only black administrator in the system was the principal of Rockmart High School, Marvin. I went and met with Marvin and asked if he would please hire me the following year. I was sick of being treated like a second-class citizen by Leanne. Ironically, the principal didn't bother me. She only intervened when Leanne sought her out. Marvin informed me that he had an agriculture position I could have. I was ecstatic and finally looked forward to the next year.

Unbelievably, midyear, the superintendent resigned; and Marvin was promoted to superintendent. I was devastated because I didn't want to teach at Rockmart High school if he wasn't going to be there. My saving grace at CMS was my students. The students were awesome and definitely had my back. I wanted to host a spaghetti dinner to give out CRCT (Criterion-Referenced Competency Tests) materials to the students and the parents. I made plans for 200 parents and students to attend. This one teacher informed me that I only needed to plan for 20 people because the parents and students would not come to *my* program. She all but said in so many words that it was because I was black.

Determined to prove her wrong, I went to my classroom and told each of my classes about my plans for the dinner. I also told them, without calling the other teacher's name, that I had been advised not to plan for more than 20 people because they supposedly wouldn't come out to the school for me. The students assured me that they would be supporting me and told me to go ahead and plan for 200 people. They also planned a program and made sure the participants represented all of our ethnicities. A couple of days before the program *I had planned and paid for*, Leanne came to my classroom and informed me that my principal would be giving the welcome, and she would be participating on the program as well.

My program, which I had been working on for a couple of weeks, was literally high jacked!

Some of the parents wanted me to stop them from taking over the program, but I explained to them that it was for the kids, so I was fine.

When the night of the program arrived, I couldn't wait to count the number of people who showed up. I didn't have 200 people in attendance, but I was pretty close with 180. I was somewhat glad the other 20 people hadn't shown up, or there would not have been enough spaghetti.

I didn't even get a plate.

Marvin called me after the program to congratulate me on it being a success. He also let me know that my principal had presented it to the board of education. Now, I understood why the program was taken over by them. I informed Marvin that I sponsored the program with my own funds. He had not realized this beforehand and informed me that he was going to have my principal reimburse me my money. Instead of getting cash from her, I asked her to buy me a class set of *Curriculum Associate* books for my students to use, which she did.

By mid-April, my principal and Leanne finally discovered that I would not be at their school the following year. The two of them should have been happy that I would not be teaching for them anymore, but they seemed upset for some reason.

The Virginia Tech shootings occurred that mid-

April, and the students and I were discussing the incident in my class after we had finished testing. A paraprofessional from another class, who was proctoring, was in the room with us. According to Leanne, the paraprofessional reported that I made a remark which appeared to be threatening.

I was flabbergasted. In all my years of teaching, I had never been accused of causing any harm or wanting to cause anyone any harm. I couldn't believe they were taking the accusation seriously. Then Marvin informed me that I was on leave with pay and couldn't return until I got a psychological evaluation. First, I was a maid/slave, and now I was an angry black crazy-psycho. Wow! Only in Northwest Georgia!

I was disappointed with Marvin at that point for acting on something he should have known was unbelievable-even after the students had given statements that I did not say anything which could be viewed as threatening. I firmly believed our superintendent, who had recently retired, would have laughed in the assistant principal's face and gone on about his business. Of course, the black superintendent wanted to be overly cautious, so it didn't appear as if he was showing favoritism to one of his own. That was the only downfall of working with weak blacks in authority. Their fear was usually detrimental to the blacks around them.

I decided since they were paying me, I would be happy to see a shrink and enjoy my paid vacation. I was happy to have a few days away from the assistant principal from hell.

The shrink gave me a clean bill of health and assured Marvin that I was harmless, just impulsive which was quite normal for ADHD (Attention Deficit Hyperactivity Disorder) adults. I was grateful for the mini vacation; I was about to graduate from the University of Georgia with my doctorate and the time off had enabled me to finish up some last-minute edits.

One would think that with only a few weeks left of school, and my impending departure near, that Leanne would simply settle down for the remainder of the year. The opposite occurred. After another disruption of my class, I finally put her in her place. My students said it was about time I stopped her from disrespecting me.

I thought nothing else of the incident until Marvin informed me that he was filing a Georgia Professional Standards Commission (GAPSC) complaint against me. Furious didn't come close to describing how I felt. In all my years of teaching, I had never had anyone try to attack my credentials.

I was now Dr. McCluskey, the only person in the building with a doctorate; and the only person in the building with a pending GAPSC case for insubordination. I reckoned I was going to need a shrink after all, for I was suddenly severely depressed.

I couldn't even be mad at Marvin. While he had submitted the complaint to the GAPSC, he gave me a contract for the next year, which rarely happened if a complaint had been sent to the GAPSC. He also made good on his promise to let me go to Rockmart High School and teach agriculture. I still couldn't believe Leanne had been so vindictive as to come for my teaching certificate with trumped-up charges. Apparently filing GAPSC complaints was not uncommon in the Polk School District. Whatever the case was, I knew I wasn't going down without a fight.

My time at Rockmart High was short lived. I already didn't feel comfortable being there and experienced a sense of uneasiness being there without the direct leadership of Marvin, my (would have been) principal who was now the superintendent. Then I discovered I was pregnant again. Blanche and McKenzie were only one and three, respectively. As if things couldn't get any worse, my husband received orders deploying him to Iraq for nine months. I took that as my cue to get the hell out of Cedartown. I was heartbroken to see my husband deploying to the Middle East again, but his leaving was the perfect excuse for me to run to my hometown and safe haven – Dixie, Georgia.

It took me two years to fight the GAPSC complaint that was filed against me. The testimony of my students and their parents exonerated me completely. Ironically, I received the news that I had been cleared of all charges on my birthday. Of course, it was the best birthday present ever!

VALDOSTA CITY

By the grace of God, I got a job at Newbern Middle School in Valdosta, Georgia. It was the beginning of September, and they were still looking for a science teacher. Initially, the principal was hesitant to hire me because of the Georgia Professional Standards Commission (GAPSC) case pending from Cedartown. Dr. Sherrell Newton, the eighth-grade assistant principal, had known me since I was a little girl and vouched for me. The other factor which helped me was receiving a new contract from the Polk School District allowing me to teach at Rockmart High. Thank God for Marvin. In a roundabout way, he had kept my career from folding.

The next two years were the best years of my teaching career. My assistant principal, Dr. Sherrell S. Newton, was one of the best administrators I had ever worked for since I had been teaching. Like Dr. Fowler, she supported her teachers wholeheartedly. More importantly, our eighth-grade teams were a cohesive unit, and I loved the students and teachers as if they were my family. We had countless fun times on that eighth-grade hall, and I am still extremely close with many of students, parents, and teachers and talk to them often.

My world crashed the day Dr. Newton informed me that they were moving her to the Alternative School for the 2009-2010 school year. She told me that she wanted to tell me herself before I could hear it from anyone else. I was speechless and in tears. When I first arrived at

Newbern, I was a broken woman; Dr. Newton was instrumental in helping me bounce back from a life-altering experience.

At that point, I was done. Dr. Newton had faithfully served Valdosta City Schools for thirty-three years. The principal who hired me had resigned, and our new principal, Betty, was good friends with Elmer, the superintendent. So I didn't know if Betty had requested to have her moved or if Elmer had asked her to support his decision to move her. Either way, I was now ready to leave, which I was supposed to be doing anyway. Had I known these changes were in the works, I wouldn't have asked my husband to extend his orders one more year so I could remain at Newbern for another school term. I had also wanted to stay near my mom another year, because my son, Derrick, was still a baby.

I vividly remember telling Dr. Newton, "If you are leaving, then I am leaving, too. I don't want to stay here without you."

She assured me, "Dr. McCluskey, it's going to be all right."

I said, "No … it's not. Everything is going to change without you."

Dr. Newton was always so regal and calm. She was typically the voice of reason and usually the most rational person in the room. There was never any chaos when she was around. What I loved most about her was the fact that she was one of the most selfless administrators I had ever worked for during my entire teaching career. She not only ensured that her students' well-being was taken care of, but she also made sure her teachers were taken care of as well. She could sense if one of her teachers was having a bad day and would offer to cover our classes and allow us to go home to regroup. Dr. Newton never operated as if she had a point to prove; she was genuine. I would often joke with her that I wanted to be like her when I grew up.

"You'll be fine," she reassured me.

I said, "I think I am going to go ahead and move to Maryland with Will."

She reminded me, "Dr. McCluskey, you are Teacher of the Year for this upcoming year. You can't disappoint your peers."

It was funny how I had forgotten about being named Teacher of the Year. After receiving the devastating news about Dr. Newton's transfer, the honor just didn't seem relevant or important after that.

I was livid when I heard who was replacing Dr. Newton as the eight-grade administrator. Our new principal, adding insult to injury, replaced Dr. Newton with the individual who had been transferred to Newbern a year earlier for disciplinary reasons. Apparently, Gomer had an affair with one of his teachers, and when news of the illicit relationship reached the central office; Elmer demoted him from principal to assistant principal. Gomer was the administrator who should have been moved to the alternative school, but I guess that is what happens when you have the complexion for protection. You will be taken care of no matter what you do. Dr. Newton's transfer was a grave injustice to the teachers and students on the eighth-grade hall. Gomer rarely left his office. Whenever we passed by his office, Gomer would always be reared back in his chair, reading a newspaper or magazine. It was beyond obvious that he didn't give a rat's ass about our school, teachers, or students. He was just at Newbern biding his time until he would be promoted to principal again, which was only a few years later. Fast forward seven years later and Gomer is now a central office administrator. Thankfully Elmer retired some years back.

I am glad I stuck around another year because, at the end of my last year at Newbern, the district decided to implement a Reduction in Force (RIF). Even the best were not immune to the RIF. Now I was about to become a troublemaker for real, and their decision to RIF Dr. Newton elevated my trouble making to a higher level.

Of course, Dr. Newton assured me everything would be all right, but I was determined to fight for her job. My intent was not to be a hero of any kind. For me this fight was about loyalty. I was going to be loyal to an individual who had been more than loyal to me. Dr. Newton had my back when I needed someone the most, and I was determined to have hers as well.

How in the world do you RIF someone with as many years of experience as Doc had? There was absolutely no rhyme or reason to their RIF process. It was as if the principals and superintendent had made a list of people who were not puppets to the system, or had brought about awareness of the district's wrongdoings, and decided to RIF them. If I had not submitted my letter of resignation, I am certain my name would have been on the list as well. I immediately asked to be placed on the board's agenda and created the website thenakedtruth4education.com which I used as my platform to expose the truths about Valdosta City Schools. I was determined to tear the system's budget apart line by line and post my suggestions as to how they could save money without implementing a RIF.

I can't remember how much the system charged me for my Freedom of Information Act (FOIA) request, but it was quite substantial. I didn't care; I just thanked God for FOIA. I finally received their line item budget, and I was determined to find the money needed to save Dr. Newton's position. I can't remember exactly when I spoke before the board the first time, but I believe it was in March or April. I explained to the board members that our system was a family, and families take care of each other. I informed them that their RIF policy was unfair and there were other ways they could make their budget balance without reducing personnel. I closed by informing the board that I would be attending every meeting they had between then and the start of school to try and persuade them to change their minds.

By the third meeting I attended, there was a crowd. The word had gotten around that I was fighting for my colleagues' jobs. I had also posted quite a bit of the budget information on my website as well. The previous school year, the system spent $14K on a fence for the baseball field at the high school, $40K for acoustics in the high school's auditorium, and $100K for a grading program. I never could figure out why so much was spent on a program that we were not using. These were just a few of the excessive expenses included in the budget. It appeared my discoveries, and subsequent posts struck a chord with Elmer.

I was summoned to the superintendent's office. Elmer asked, "What do I need to do to make your website disappear?"

I replied, "You know what needs to be done."

"You want me to give those people their jobs back?"

"Yes, sir! If you do that, I will delete the entire website and not blog another word."

Dr. Newton called me later on in the week and informed me that everyone was getting their job back. I was seriously annoyed because instead of restoring her back her administrative position, Elmer had assigned her to an English classroom. Technically, he had kept his word, so I kept mine and deleted my site.

Dr. Newton decided to retire after that year. She didn't get to stay with the school system as long as she wanted, but what she received was far more precious – time to spend with her family, including a vacation to Paris, France. Little did we know that she wouldn't be with us much longer.

As I sat at her funeral in December 2013, I was at peace. Although my good friend was gone, and I wouldn't be able to talk with her for hours any longer, I had gained a guardian angel to watch over me. When I decided to step out on faith and finally walk away from public education, I believed in my heart that if Dr. Newton was still here, she would have assured me, "Dr. McCluskey, it is going to be alright."

It seemed as if my last year in Valdosta was battle ridden. Now that I am looking back, I think I was so irritated at the mistreatment of Dr. Newton-I was ready to fight any and all injustices in my path. My next battle with Valdosta City was regarding the disenfranchisement of black students, who had been previously retained. I don't even think the board was aware of the new policy, which stated that any student who was going to be 16 by the ninth grade had to attend the Pinevale Learning Center (PLC). These kids could not even step foot into our high school. When Betty asked us to identify these kids, I asked, "Are you guys serious about this?"

At that time, they had made the PLC a separate school so their test scores would not count against the middle and high schools. Therefore, if they dumped these kids over at the PLC, their scores wouldn't hurt the middle or high school scores. Furthermore, the kids wouldn't be able to negatively impact the graduation rate either.

It's amazing how systems can manipulate data to

make it seem as if non-existent progress is being made. I didn't realize, until four years ago, my address to the BOE from that night had been captured by a blogger. My MacIntyre (Thomasville City) coworkers brought it to my attention that the new librarian had uncovered it while trying to dig up information on me. For some reason she was fascinated by me. One of the board members had called me a troublemaker. He didn't realize that I had a pretty good relationship with another board member who told me what he had said about me. I addressed his comment first and then shared my concerns with the board:

> *I want to address this first. I know some of you probably say that I am a troublemaker, and I have thought long and hard about this. Before I came before you guys, I did some soul-searching, and I said, You know what? Harriet Tubman, I am sure, was a troublemaker, and Martin L. King, Jr., and Malcolm X, Sojourner Truth, Rosa Parks, Dr. Dorothy Heights, and I am sure Leigh Touchton and Beverly Madison are also troublemakers. I am pretty sure the biggest troublemaker of them all right now is probably President Barack Obama. The one thing I can say is this: If it had not been for these troublemakers, I would not have been able to walk through the front door of the Valdosta City School Board (VCSB), and I would not be able to stand here before you tonight holding a doctorate from the University of Georgia. So, if my troublemaking will make a change in the Valdosta City School System—guys, I am sorry, but I am*

going to have to make a little more trouble. I want you to see that I am not trying to work against you. I just want change to come.

The emphatics for initiating this awareness began in my classroom, and most people don't know this. My students and I would go to the newspaper, and we would pull out articles. We looked at the crime section. We looked for those students—those people who were 25 and below. We clipped out the articles, posted them and discussed them. We realized something quickly; most of those people were people we knew. Most of those people were people who had dropped out of the Valdosta City School System, and my goal was to do something. We had to make a change.

One of us could have been that person sitting in the Waffle House refusing to give up our wallet to somebody the Valdosta City School System failed. And that's the bottom line. That's the biggest point most people do not understand. It's not whether or not we like each other—ah, I like y'all by the way, but it's not all about whether we like each other; it's about doing what is right for kids.

What I want to talk about with you tonight is a policy that I am sure you guys don't know about. Last year, we were instructed to send our old students to the PLC. As eighth grade teachers, we had to identify students that were going to be 16 in the ninth grade. We ended up sending 17 students I know from the eighth grade who did not go to the high school. The seventh-grade teachers identified 20 students, and our sixth-grade teachers identified 15 students. What happened is that we ended up sending 52 students to the PLC. Now I had a problem with that because the next thing that came up was the PLC was a separate school now. The first thing I said was, Oh, my God. They are going to dump kids over there because those test scores would not count. When I looked at the test scores this time—of course, that's what happened. Every last one of those 22 ninth graders that took the math tests at the PLC failed. So, my thing is this—I have a question, and I am hoping one of you will answer it. Why was the Pineville Learning Center turned into a regular school? And why is it that we had 52 students and Valdosta Middle School only had four. You know it would not be bad if you sent them over there and were going to do something special for them like come up with something innovative to get them learning. But it's not equal over there.

They have fewer resources than both middle schools. I know I sent an e-mail to a board member saying this is ridiculous. These kids are using this textbook; this science textbook that we threw away this year and discontinued two years ago. After I fussed and balked a little bit, they finally got science textbooks—brand new science textbooks. I know because I pulled them out of my closet and sent them over there. They got workbooks, finally. I had five computers, and when I would go over to work with science teachers at the PLC, I felt so bad because here I was sitting with five computers. I could do WEB QUESTs, and at that time, they had only one.

So, I am begging you tonight ... if you are going

to dump them at the PLC, then at least take time out of your busy schedule and go over to the PLC. This is something that you need to see for yourself because you know they say women lie; men lie, but numbers don't lie. Go see it for yourself, and you will see that the items are not there. You will see what textbooks they have and don't have. This made me think about the school my mom used to talk about back in the 60s, and I, really, really feel that if you are concerned, and if you are interested, please go over there and do something for our kids. It's kind of sad because people [male board members] are looking at their watches and things.

I am going to be honest with you, a change is not going to come until you are ready for a change to come, and if you are not ready to do right by the kids of Valdosta, then you will not see a change in Valdosta. The crime will continue to go up and pretty soon, it will be over to Creekside, on the other side of town, and then it will be too late. Thank you!

Ironically, one of my former principals, Mr. Keith Hose, is now the new principal of Valdosta's alternative school, which has been renamed Maceo A. Horne Learning Center (HLC). The old Pinevale Learning Center (PLC) no longer exists; a new elementary school, Pinevale Elementary, was built on the land once occupied by the PLC. The HLC is housed in one of Valdosta's old elementary schools and is no longer classified as a separate school; it is again an alternative program that serves Valdosta High, Newbern Middle, and Valdosta Middle School. I visited the program in November 2017 and was quite pleased by what I witnessed. Principal Hose and Dr. Virginia Crowell, assistant principal, seemed to manage the school very well.

2 EDUCATION UP NORTH

When I left Valdosta, I accompanied my husband to his next duty station in Aberdeen, Maryland. It's somewhat sad that I am about to give this advice: Until public schools implement programs which promote student success and improve student learning, I encourage anyone who is moving to another city, town, or state to check the status of the educational system first, and then purchase or rent a home based on what you discover.

Before I rented a house in Aberdeen, I checked out the Harford County School System first. Our oldest son, Se'von, was in high school; McKenzie was in first; Blanche was in Pre-K, and Derrick was attending daycare.

There are approximately 20 elementary schools in Harford County, so location is important. A little over

700 students attended the elementary school I ultimately selected. Though it wasn't as small as I wanted, I was impressed with the ratings for Church Creek Elementary. I am not a fan of large elementary schools because a child's early learning experiences are most influential in a child's future and students may be easily overlooked if the population is too great. It's far easier for kids to slip through the cracks when too many kids attend.

I also loved the fact that Church Creek Elementary was quite diverse. The ratio of white students to students of other ethnicities was almost 50/50. After the discrimination I had endured in the Polk County School District, I was determined that my kids not experience being the only minority student in their classes until they were older and mature enough to tackle any obstacles they would possibly face.

I found us a home, less than two miles from the school, on Winners Circle in Belcamp, Maryland. Thank God, my husband was a military officer, which allowed us to receive BAH (Basic Allowance for Housing) to cover the $1800 rent. The house was two stories and had a basement; it was in immaculate condition. My landlord was a local teacher who had just recently divorced and was downsizing for two years until she was able to get back on her feet. We thought it was a brilliant idea for her to rent her house to us for two years and then move back in when we left Maryland to retire for good. Most people would have simply foreclosed, but she didn't do that and is now happily back in her beautiful home.

I didn't attempt to get a teaching position in Harford County, mainly because I knew Maryland had a strong teacher union that protected its teachers. The union provided job stability for teachers, lessening the likelihood of available positions. To prepare for the possibility of not having a job, I had enrolled in Webster University months earlier and began pursuing a Master's Degree in Procurement. If nothing else, I was going to prepare myself to become a federal employee and find a job at Aberdeen Proving Ground, which I did.

McKenzie loved her new school, and I loved her new teacher, Mrs. Tammy Greenwood. Mrs. Greenwood was from New Jersey and a hell of a teacher. My baby blossomed while in her class. I enjoyed working with Mrs. Greenwood so much that year I begged her to switch grades so she could teach my daughter Blanche also. I don't know if she was allowed to move grades because of my request, but she did move down to kindergarten, and I was ecstatic. Foundations are extremely important in education, and I sincerely believe that Mrs. Greenwood provided a strong foundation for my babies.

While waiting for my federal job to come to fruition, I became a Harford County substitute teacher and accepted a long-term position as a family and consumer science teacher at their alternative school. The first day I reported to the alternative school, I initially thought I had gone to the wrong school. My son was attending Aberdeen High School next door, so I knew I had to have been in the correct place.

When the secretary informed me that I was at their alternative school, I almost fainted.

I know I probably sounded dumb when I asked, "Y'all got white kids?"

Not only did they have white kids, they had a lot of them. This was unlike any alternative school I had been in back home in the South where almost every student was black. This school had a hundred or so students, which is not bad at all for a system that has 37,000 students. Most of the kids were assigned to this setting temporarily, typically a semester, for minor infractions committed at their home schools. I don't remember anyone in my class being assigned to this program for longer than a year.

What astounded me most about this school was how the place functioned like a traditional school. There were teachers in each class, and they taught the students their assignments. In most of the alternative programs in the state of Georgia, students are required to stare at a computer screen all day and complete computerized lessons. These kids were provided opportunities to engage in meaningful activities they seemed to enjoy.

My classroom had a fully functioning kitchen, and the students and I used it daily. Surprisingly, I wasn't expected to purchase any supplies or food with my personal funds. Everything was provided for the class. The end of the semester was bittersweet because I had started to fall in love with the school.

I left the alternative school and started a new job working as a secretary for the Department of Defense's C4SIR (Command, Control, Communications, Computers, Intelligence, Surveillance and Reconnaissance) organization. I will have to write a follow-up book to describe my experiences as a military spouse working with the federal government. Without giving too much away, I will say it was a very interesting experience. I was awarded C4SIR Employee of the Year for 2012, so I guess I didn't step on too many toes.

We lived in Maryland for three years before returning to Georgia, and my daughters attended the public school system there the entire time. My experiences with my son's matriculation were far different. Whereas my daughters were winning awards for their behavior in school, my sons had not reached that level of distinction.

Derrick was wreaking havoc at the daycare, and Se'von was upsetting one of his teachers at Aberdeen High School by constantly laying his head on his desk.

When parents say, "They don't act like that with me at the house."

I now believe them.

My boys didn't act like that with me, just with other adults when I was not around. My only saving grace was how pleasant my girls were, and they lived in the same house as the boys. So their behavior couldn't be blamed solely on our parenting.

I hired a nanny, Ms. Jamie Toney, a native of

Harford County to watch Derrick for me at our house. She was a godsend, and Derrick knew not to play with Ms. Jamie. After a couple of months, Ms. Jamie and Derrick both started going to Brighter Beginnings Child Care in Aberdeen. Ms. Vanessa, the owner, was a friend of Ms. Jamie's. She allowed Derrick to attend, and Ms. Jamie worked for her as well. It was the perfect set up for all of us.

I gave Se'von an ultimatum: he could either get himself together or I was going to pull him out of public school. I refused to deal with him being oppositional defiant toward his teachers any longer. I knew he wasn't sleeping in class and was positive he heard every word his teacher said while his head was down on his desk. He knew this was a pet peeve of his teacher's and was repeatedly placing his head on the desk to aggravate her.

Se'von had always been good at exploiting the weakest link during his tenure in middle and high school. Unfortunately, he had not adjusted well to our moving all of the time. By the time he made friends, our two years were up, and we were off to our next duty station. The constant moving made him wary of trying to form any long-term relationships. Whereas I had made tons of friends all across Georgia, Florida, Maryland and in between, he made very few; I don't think he still talks to anyone from his past today.

I will never forget the day that his teacher called to inform me that once again Se'von had his head down. Se'von was a junior at Aberdeen High and thankfully, the first semester was coming to an end. I thanked his teacher for calling me and drove over to the school. I planned to keep my promise to withdraw him from school.

By the time I reached Aberdeen High, I was no longer angry; but, I still hadn't changed my mind. Today was going to be Se'von's last day in the building. I asked the secretary to direct me to the counselor's office so that I could withdraw my son. The counselor was shocked that I was removing him from school and asked me what I was going to do with him. I replied with something to the effect that since Se'von didn't feel he needed to follow his teacher's directions, then he was grown, and grown people didn't go to high school.

I know the counselor thought I had lost my everlasting mind. My assumption was confirmed when she directed me to the principal's office. He pleaded with me not to withdraw Se'von from school. I think he was more concerned that withdrawing Se'von without a transfer would be coded as a drop out in the school's data. I assured him that Se'von was not going to be sitting at my house, and he could code him as going to college.

Now, I know they thought I was seriously cuckoo.

By this time, Se'von had reached the principal's office; he was shocked that I was there. His shock evolved into tears when he realized I was making good on my promise to withdraw him from school.

"I don't want to be a dropout," he begged me.

"You should have thought about that before you put your head down again on your desk." I had warned him that one more phone call from that teacher was going to result in serious consequences.

I was done.

We got in the car and started driving. After several miles, Se'von realized that we were not going home, but he didn't say anything. When we finally arrived at Harford Community College, he asked, "Why are we here?

I turned, looked at him, and said, "Se'von, you are grown. Grown people don't go to high school; they go to college."

His eyes became big as saucers. He couldn't believe I was about to enroll him in college.

"I'm going to college?" he asked.

"Yes, sir!" I assured him. "You are going to college."

"But I don't have a high school diploma."

"Doesn't matter. All you need is a G.E.D."

I planned to have Se'von take the **G.E.D. (General Equivalency Diploma test)**, which I was certain he would pass with flying colors. My son was naturally smart and absorbed information with ease. He reminded me of one of my former classmates. While everyone else in Brooks County High college prep classes was studying our behinds off, he breezed through everything! All he had to do was listen, and he got it.

When we got to Harford Community College, I

explained to the Admissions Counselor that I wanted my son to take his GED. I said I didn't think high school was challenging enough for him. Rather than have him complete the second semester of his eleventh-grade year of high school, I thought he was ready for college. The counselor was extremely supportive and explained the entire GED process to me. I knew what a GED was; but honestly, I had never personally known anyone who had completed the process. It wasn't until I became a graduation coach, several years later, that I realized I had made the best decision for my son. Ironically, if we had still been in Georgia, he could have participated in dual enrollment, but I honestly don't think Maryland had that option at the time in 2012. If they did, no one at Aberdeen High School had shared that information with me.

Recently, I went to Harford Community College's website and noticed that there are numerous Early College Admissions (ECA) options available to the students of Harford County. They can be dually enrolled (take college classes and use the credits for both high school and college); concurrently enrolled (take classes beyond the regular school day and choose not to use them for high school credit, but earn regular college credit); and waive their senior year (complete their senior year at HCC and when 24 college-level credits are earned, receive a high school diploma). It appears that in 2013, the State of Maryland passed Senate Bill 740 which allows their high school students to do all of the above. The goal of the bill:

> Establish curriculum and graduation requirements aimed at college readiness and completion in the state of Maryland. Further, it is the goal of the state that at least 55 percent of Maryland adults age 25 to 64 will hold at least an associate's degree by the year 2025.

What an outstanding goal!

That day we signed my son up to take the college placement exam and the GED test. The plan was for him to take college courses, and I would pay for them until his GED scores came back. Because he didn't have a high school diploma, he didn't qualify for the Pell Grant; however, once he passed the GED, he would then become eligible for financial aid.

Se'von passed his entrance test in English with ease, but the math was as we expected – was challenging. He hated math and had hated the subject all of his life. His hatred of math hadn't started until the fourth grade. I think it began as a result of him refusing to learn his multiplication tables.

It was extremely important for children to learn their multiplication tables prior to or during their third grade year. Most of the students I had encountered who hated math, hated the subject because they had never learned their basic facts. After third grade, multiplication is an integral part of math, and it's hard for students to function without knowing their multiplication facts.

The poor math scores didn't keep him from being able to attend college; it just meant that he would have to take a developmental studies type class before he could take the regular MAT101 course. We decided he would start with three classes, and I can't remember how much they cost exactly, but I know it wasn't much more than a thousand dollars. The costly textbooks stunned me more than that of tuition. Still, I love technical colleges and think they are the best-kept secrets. I plan to send both of my daughters to one beginning their tenth-grade year. It's sheer craziness not to get an Associate's degree while in high school. That is two years of college that I won't have to pay for. I'll discuss dual enrollment in more details in a later chapter.

I wasn't worried that Se'von would have problems in college. College is a great place for oppositional people. Having options and being given choices is the best treatment for dealing with oppositional defiant individuals. College students can choose their schedules, teachers, and courses, which is an oppositional person's dream.

After the first day of class, Se'von was super excited! He rushed in the house and couldn't wait to tell me about his day. One thing he said to me that I never forgot was, "Momma, all black boys who drop out or want to drop out need to go to college!"

Perplexed, I asked, "Why?"

He began by explaining the freedom he enjoyed in selecting his seat in class. Then he went on to tell me how he was able to sit anywhere he wanted to in the class. He was able to go to the restroom without having to get a pass or ask for permission. No one was in his classroom acting silly or goofing off, and the teacher encouraged the students to participate in classroom dialogue.

He was in heaven, and so was I.

We didn't get Se'von's GED scores back until late April. To my utter dismay, by this time, he had decided that he would rather pursue a career in the Army. He had been to the local station, met with a recruiter, and enlisted. All he needed now were his GED scores, and he would be able to complete the process. I tried to persuade him to complete a four-year degree first and then enlist as an officer as his dad had done, but he was adamant that he was ready to move on to greener pastures.

Se'von's GED scores were phenomenal. Even sweeter was the fact that Maryland awards a high school diploma if a person's GED score is 410 or higher on each of the five tests and an average standard score of 450 on all of the five tests. Se'von scored a 710 in Language Arts/Writing, 800 in Social Studies, 710 in Science, 700 in Language Arts/Reading, and a 550 in Mathematics. We figured the mathematics score would probably be lower than the others, but it still was higher than average. Except for the 69th percentile rank in math, Se'von ranked in the 98th percentile and higher on all of his other test scores. As I figured, high school was not challenging enough for him. Now instead of wasting his time in high school for another year, Se'von had obtained his high school diploma and would be serving his country in the United States Army.

It wasn't until we returned to Georgia that I realized how vastly different the educational systems in Maryland and Georgia were. Various polls rank public education systems. Despite Maryland's shifting position in the polls, it seems to always be ranked in the Top 20. Georgia can be found in the mid to low 30s. In the 2017 HuffPost poll that ranks public education systems by state, Maryland was ranked #5 and Georgia #32. The difference in these rankings was evident upon our return.

3 BACK IN GEORGIA

Around June 2013, my husband was given orders to deploy to Afghanistan. This deployment was his third; his first two stints had been in Iraq. Since he would be gone for longer than six months, we decided it would be best for the kids and me to go ahead and move back to my hometown, Dixie, Georgia. This decision was made even easier on the account of my husband being scheduled to have ankle surgery upon his return from overseas and would be on terminal leave until his retirement a few months later. We didn't want our kids to have to change schools midyear. Eventually, we were going to move back to my husband's hometown, Cedartown, Georgia, because we had built our retirement home there in 2006. For the most part, I was fine with the decision.

My work for the federal government during the past

three years had been quite challenging and rewarding. It shocked me when I was awarded C4SIR Employee of the Year for 2012. I knew I had done a great job working for Army Contracting Command, but I had also given them hell on numerous occasions about not treating their military spouses fairly; thus, I was indeed surprised that they had not held any of my troublemaking against me.

McKenzie and Blanche settled into Quitman Elementary with no problems. Despite being gone for three years, the girls still had friends in the school system and picked up where they left off. Derrick, Jr. was another story altogether.

Derrick was beginning his first year of kindergarten. For a week or so, we thought everything was going to be okay. However, we were greatly mistaken. Before the first month of school was over, Derrick was suspended. I had never in my life seen a kindergartener suspended from school. I spanked him for getting into trouble and thought things would get better. They became far worse. It soon became a pattern that Derrick attended school on Monday, Tuesday, and Wednesday and being suspended for Thursday and Friday.

When I left Maryland I knew I would be reentering the teaching profession. I missed it so much; however, Derrick was having such a hard time transitioning to kindergarten that I delayed trying to find another teaching position. Even though he had attended daycare in Maryland, Derrick had never attended a formal Pre-K program like the girls had, and I could tell the difference.

At the end of August 2013, I started looking for teaching positions. I didn't dream of going near Valdosta because I was still pissed at how they had treated Dr. Newton. Furthermore, I didn't quite trust their new superintendent, Elmer's predecessor, either. I don't know exactly what caused his demise, but he only lasted two years before he abruptly resigned that February. Karma most certainly is a bitch.

To make myself more marketable as I traveled to different duty stations with my husband, I became certified in all areas of middle grades (4-8), agriculture (6-12), and family and consumer science (6-12). So, I knew finding a position wouldn't be too difficult even though the school year had already begun. I noticed that Thomasville City had an opening for a middle school reading teacher and decided to apply.

I searched their website and noticed that Mrs. Courtney Almond, one of my coworkers from Newbern Middle School, was now teaching at MacIntyre Park. I called Courtney and asked her about the school. She was excited that I was back in Georgia and suggested that I apply. Next, I called the principal, Mr. Keith Hose, and told him I was interested in his reading position, and he asked me to come in for an interview.

When I arrived at MacIntyre, I was shocked to discover the building was brand new. I had ridden by the school numerous times before I had moved to Maryland and had no idea that they had built a brand new two-story addition. While waiting for Mr. Hose, one of the teachers brought a student to the front office. The little girl looked more like she was in elementary school than middle. The teacher was livid, and despite not knowing who I was, she continued arguing with the student until the secretary intervened. The secretary instructed the teacher to return to her class, where the students she had left unsupervised were waiting. She told the girl to sit in the waiting area, where I was seated. It was clear that the student was agitated, and she was not letting the matter go quickly.

After the little girl settled into a seat next to mine, I struck up a conversation with her to ease the tension. I asked, "What's your name?"

"Jade," she said still visibly upset.

"What grade are you in?" I probed further.

She replied, "Sixth."

"Oh, boy," I thought. I was there to apply for the sixth-grade reading teacher position, which meant I would have to teach her.

Finally, curious as to who I was, Jade asked, "Why are you here?"

"I'm here applying for the sixth-grade reading teacher job."

"That's my grade."

"I know."

"What's going on with your teacher and you?" I asked her.

"She doesn't like me," Jade huffed, "She is always kicking me out!"

"What do you do for her to kick you out?" I asked.

"Nothing," she reassured me, "I honestly don't do nothing." I didn't press the issue because I noticed the conversation was making Jade become agitated again.

"Are you a mean teacher?" she asked me.

I looked at her and smiled, "Only if my students turn my meanness on."

She laughed.

"What church do you attend?" I asked her.

Jade shrugged her shoulders. I figured that meant she didn't attend a particular church.

"I do go sometimes," she told me.

"Well I want you to watch how you behave young lady," I encouraged her, "God is watching you. You do know He sees what you are doing?"

Before she could answer the question, Mr. Hose came from the back to get me. He stopped in his tracks when he saw me talking to Jade.

He raised his eyebrows.

Jade was about to start back up, but I shook my head and whispered, "Chill out. If you embarrass this man in front of me, he's going to send you home for a few days. It's not worth it."

She took a deep breath and sat back.

I winked at her, smiled, stood up, and extended my hand to Mr. Hose.

I said, "I'm Dr. McCluskey, and I genuinely think I can be an asset to you."

He interviewed me for about thirty minutes and told me I had the job. Now all I had to do was go to the central office to complete an application.

JIM CROW

I often tell people that Thomasville, Georgia, has not gotten the memo. Of course, they ask, "What memo?"

I reply, "The memo that Jim Crow is over!"

Thomasville City Schools was one of the most segregated school systems I had ever worked in. They had three elementary schools; two were predominately black, and one was predominately white. I would think that with only one middle school and one high school, it would be a grueling task to segregate students. It was until Thomasville became creative and opened their Scholar's Academy. By the time, I began working for Mr. Hose in 2012, all but four of the system's white middle school students attended the Scholar's Academy. There were two white males in the eighth grade, and I had two white females in my sixth-grade class.

I was dumbfounded and couldn't quite understand what in the world was going on in Thomasville City Schools. A private school had been created within the public school system! It dawned on me that in 2006, when the Scholar's Academy was created, our country was in the midst of a bad recession. In my estimation, white students who formerly attended private school had to return to the public school system due to financial constraints. The creation of the Scholar's Academy solved their problems. These affluent kids could attend the public school system without having to associate with those students from low socioeconomic backgrounds since the Scholar's Academy was mostly comprised of whites, upper-class blacks, and teachers' kids for the most part.

Sadly, in addition to encouraging blatant segregation, this so-called special program also wasted taxpayers' dollars in regards to the unnecessary positions it created. According to open.georgia.gov for the 2017 school year, their principal was paid $92,760.28; assistant principal $80,176.70; two counselors $121,956.84, and receptionist $22,800.94. This program duplicated positions found in the two traditional schools, and this duplication costs big time—$317,694.76 each year to be exact.

Jim Crow failed miserably the first time because the powers to be didn't quite grasp the concept of separate but equal. They understood separate very well but never comprehended what the term equal encompassed. It is my genuine belief that if our governmental leaders had sincerely understood the implications of equal during Jim Crow, we would probably still be separated now. It is my strong conviction that had blacks been provided the same facilities and resources as their white counterparts, black would have been content to continue teaching and learning with their own. For instance, the elementary school building that I was educated in (grade K-7) was a fairly nice brick structure. When the school system informed our community that the schools were consolidating, we were heartbroken and didn't want to merge. I must admit, if we had been housed in a subpar structure, we probably would have wanted to move to something better.

Those in charge had learned from their past mistakes. This time around, instead of making black students attend rundown, substandard, poorly built facilities, those in power were building fabulous million-dollar facilities to house their students of color, and this new tactic was working. Now it appeared as if black and white students were being treated equally, but this was not the case in many instances. Many systems were becoming creative like Thomasville and creating special "academies" to separate students based on race, and no one was saying much about it.

There was little resistance because people were being blinded by the beautiful new facilities.

When I started my first year in Thomasville City, I taught in a brand new multimillion-dollar facility that my students and parents loved because of its appearance. The community failed to realize that while the black kids were being educated in this brand-new facility, the course offerings that their children received vastly differed from those being offered to the Scholar's Academy students.

Our students were being taught basic academics and only offered three enrichment courses: physical education, music, and band. The last being a joint venture between the two schools. On the other hand, the students at the Scholar's Academy were offered dance classes (facilitated through the cultural center located next door), studio art, business/computer science, strings, theatre, drama tech, broadcast video, agriculture, and Spanish.

It was most disturbing to witness how different the black students were treated in comparison to their white counterparts. When our students changed classes, they had to quietly stand next to the wall in a straight line outside their classroom door - like prisoners.

Their counterparts did not.

Our students had to walk to the lunchroom, which is outside of the main building, in a straight line.

Their counterparts did not.

Our students were mandated to eat in the cafeteria in assigned seats.

Their counterparts were allowed to eat lunch outside or in their café area, which consisted of booths, tables, and liberated space. When it rained, they would come in the cafeteria and take our students' assigned seats and make them sit elsewhere. That was until I was hired.

On a rainy day, shortly after I was hired, our sixth-grade classes entered the cafeteria. My coworker became visibly upset and told me, "They always do this. Now we have to find our classes somewhere else to sit!"

"Why?" I asked.

"The Scholar's kids have taken our seats."

Being new, I asked, "Well, where are their assigned

seats?"

She responded, "They sit wherever they want."

"Um ... not today," I informed her and made my way to our assigned tables as our students entered the lunch line.

I cordially asked the Academy students to move to the two rows of empty tables that were opposite ours. No one ever sat at those, and they were free. The kids were very well-mannered and moved without hesitation or complaint.

Their teacher, on the other hand, was livid that I dared ask her students to move. I explained that these were the assigned seats we sat in daily and asked if she thought it was fair that our students had to move when it rained just to accommodate them.

Unbelievably, she thought that was acceptable.

I politely remarked, "I know you guys are still trying to be segregated around here, but Jim Crow is over, honey. You remember Rosa Parks? That's us. We are not giving up any seats around here anymore either."

I left her standing in the middle of the lunchroom and walked back to the table, where my coworkers were watching. I knew Mr. Hose would probably be calling me in that afternoon, which he did. Their principal had come to his office shortly after lunch to ask him about this incredulous new teacher he hired, and why was she talking about Rosa Parks.

The longer I remained at MacIntyre Park, the more aware I became of the countless *scholars* who remained identified. Many of our students were brilliant. I asked several why were they not attending the Scholar's Academy, and they replied, "It's too hard over there." I was fairly certain that my class was as rigorous as, if not more than, the courses offered at the Scholar's Academy. I had always believed in challenging students and making sure that I did so in whatever subject I taught. If students were taking my class, it was being taught at grade level and above. If students were making A's and B's in my class, they had proved they were indeed scholars.

I have never forgotten my assistant principal telling me I was being "too hard" on my students. I was teaching her son fifth-grade science at Sumter County Middle School in Americus, Georgia in 1998. Granted the fifth-grade standards didn't require the kids to know all 206 bones of the body; however, I felt they needed to learn as many as possible to make biology easier in their near future. My principal, Mrs. Carolyn Kerr-Hamilton, learned about "bone-gate" after walking by my classroom and noticing me performing the bone dance on top of my lab table. I was dancing energetically and singing my favorite part when Mrs. Kerr-Hamilton walked into my room.

"Big toe, tibia"
"Other side, fibula"

"Ms. Mitchell, exactly what are you doing?" she interrupted me, grinning from ear to ear. Mrs. Kerr-Hamilton was more like a mother to me than a principal.

She taught me a lot during my two years working for her, and I often joked with her that I owed her immensely for tolerating me during my first two years of teaching. I was most positively a diamond in the rough then. If I hadn't had to commute forty-five minutes to get to work, I would have taught for her until she retired.

I looked down at her and replied, "I'm doing the bone dance."

"The bone dance?" she asked.

"My students know almost 30 major bones of the body," I bragged.

"Do they for real?" she asked.

"Yep!" I confirmed. My students were smiling from ear to ear.

"I'll be right back," Mrs. Kerr-Hamilton said and left my classroom.

We went back to boogying!

Mrs. Kerr-Hamilton reappeared in my classroom with a life-sized skeleton from the library in tow. My students were enthusiastic to share their knowledge as she quizzed them. Mrs. Kerr-Hamilton was blown away by their knowledge, and so was I. When I taught high school biology a few years later, I understood the rigor which would be required of the students and how I had aptly prepared them for this undertaking.

After about a month at MacIntyre Park, I realized that all of the separations had hurt our kids. By housing the scholars in a separate facility, our kids were being shown they were not scholars but instead inferior. So, I came up with this bright idea which I shared with my students. I told them I needed their help to prove something. Of course, they were all ears and wanted to know what I wanted them to help me prove.

I said, "I want you guys to help me prove that we are smart, too."

They wanted to know how.

I told them I needed for each of them to pass the CRCT test when it was administered that spring. I wanted a 100 percent pass rate on the test to prove that we were just as smart as our counterparts next door.

They were hyped and accepted the challenge.

I would occasionally have to remind them when they groaned about learning new material that I needed them to have my back. Usually, that was all it took to get them motivated again.

Many of our students from low socioeconomic households, simply needed someone to encourage them and uncover their astonishing abilities. Students do as expected. If I expected them to fail, they would; if I expected them to succeed, they would. There were far too many in education now with low or no expectations, which was the root cause behind many failing schools.

My principal, Mr. Hose, and Assistant Principal, Ms. Ishia Dawson, supported my endeavors to help our school improve and our children achieve. MacIntyre Park was the first school where I started giving $20 scholarships to students who earned all A's. At our first Honor Roll celebration, I was so disappointed to see that no one had earned all A's. How can a school of more than 300 students not have one student to earn all A's? After the awards ceremony, I asked Mr. Hose if I could present a challenge to our students – a $20 bill for High Honor Roll ... all A's. He agreed and at the next assembly, he allowed me to give the honorees, though few, a $20 bill and challenge the entire student body. I joked with them, "Guys, I really want to make it rain in here!"

Our 2013 College and Career Ready Performance Index (CCRPI) score, the year prior to my coming, was a 64.1, and our school was slated to be placed on the Failing School List if we didn't make any improvements that year.

I knew we had to be creative and the incentives had to be large. Mr. Hose had academic quiz bowls to get the kids excited about learning. We came up with the 850 Club. A score of 850 meant the student exceeded on the CRCT, and our goal was to get as many 850s as possible. I purchased Amazon tablets to be given to the top female and male from each grade with the highest CRCT score, and a bicycle for each overall top scoring male and female student.

Not only did my students improve, but MacIntyre Park improved tremendously. My students certainly delivered on their promise to me! They all passed the reading portion of the CRCT to earn me a 100 percent pass rate. In addition to their passing, many earned scores of 850 and higher. It was amazing how many students worked so diligently to gain membership into the 850 Club and receive a bracelet engraved with the numbers 850. There was no way that MacIntyre Park was going to be on the failing school list in 2014, and we were not. Our 2014 CCRPI score was 77.2. The school had increased 13.1 points in one year.

I was looking forward to year two at MacIntyre Park. I wanted to see just how high we could increase our CCRPI score the upcoming year.

FAVOR CHRISTIAN ACADEMY

While everything was going great for me at MacIntyre Park, things were not going so well for Derrick, Jr. at Quitman Elementary. He was not transitioning well to public school. I could now relate to those parents who sometimes claimed in parent conferences, "My child does not act like that at home." I could now attest to the fact that some of these parents were telling the truth. My own child did not act at school as he did at home. He never refused to do what I instructed him to do or threw massive temper tantrums at home.

Daily, I was growing more and more frustrated because it seemed as if I had to leave work at least once a week to pick him up from school, and his suspensions were becoming more frequent. At that point, I had decided if I received another phone call from his school,

I was going to move Derrick from Brooks County to Thomasville where I was. I needed him in a closer vicinity, so my frequent trips to the school would be easier.

I asked my students which school would be best for him to attend in Thomasville. They told me not to allow him to go to the elementary school next door because he would probably act the same. Then one of my students suggested Favor Christian Academy which was a private Christian school owned by Dr. Linda McLean, and her husband, Ronald, who was a local physician.

The kids had become excited when they started talking about Dr. McLean.

"She will straighten him out!" one of them bellowed.

"She doesn't play," another shared.

"She's like you," yet another one told me.

I was excited. It sounded to me as if Dr. McLean's school was structured; this was what my son desperately needed.

"Now she has a ruler named Doughnut, which she uses to paddle you," one of the students warned.

"But she really doesn't use it. She just makes you think she will," another one said.

"Ooo, that's good." I smiled. Of course, they groaned.

I told them I believed in corporal punishment.

"But you said you don't whip your kids," they reminded me.

I explained that I didn't "whip" them often, but I did get their rear ends when needed. I always talked to my children because I wanted them to understand the detriment of misbehavior and to make the best decisions possible. Then we came up with a consequence for the behavior. My goal was to help them make better choices and learn from their mistakes. This worked beautifully with my girls who earned awards for their behavior. Derrick, on the other hand, seemed to be pushing the envelope toward more whippings. This was sheer craziness because he hated them. I rarely had to whip him because the mention of getting one usually stopped him in his tracks.

A few days after my conversation with the students about Favor Christian Academy, I received yet another call from Derrick's school. This particular phone call informed me there had been an incident at the school. Initially, I panicked because I thought Derrick was injured. Not only was he not injured, his behind was the perpetrator of the incident. As the principal provided me the details, I kept asking her, "Are you talking about my Derrick?"

Evidently, Derrick had become enraged after the teacher had refused to allow him to do something that he wanted to do. Instead of complying with her directives, he chose to destroy her room instead. The principal told me they had to remove all of the students from the classroom because my child was out of control and throwing things around the classroom. I let her know I was on my way and that when I got there, Derrick had better not be sitting in the office playing with a stuffed animal as he usually did.

By the time I reached Quitman Elementary, I was fuming. Derrick had undoubtedly crossed the line this time. I did not want him thinking that disrupting the learning environment was going to be at any time acceptable. I signed in and went straight to my friend Brittany's office. I knew she would tell me the truth about what was going on. As I figured, she told me that Derrick had been disruptive for quite some time at school. My girls were so good that no one even believed Derrick was related to them, let alone living in the same house with them.

As we were talking, I heard screaming in the hallway. I recognized Derrick's voice, so I peeked out of the doorway to see what was going on. The assistant principal and another individual were dragging Derrick down the hallway. He was refusing to walk, so they had to drag him. I was done with the foolishness.

I turned to Brittany and asked, "Can I please borrow your office for a few minutes?"

She said, "Sure."

I stepped fully into the hallway and revealed myself to the administrator and Derrick.

"Derrick what are you doing?" I asked.

When Derrick saw me, he acted like he had seen a ghost. He immediately jumped, like Scooby Doo, straight to his feet and started walking normally. It was too late; he was busted. I told the assistant principal that I needed to see Derrick for a moment.

He was reluctant to come into Brittany's office. Derrick could tell from my demeanor that I was very upset with him.

He kept saying, "I am sorry momma. I am sorry momma."

Brittany gathered some papers off her desk, and said, "I'll go make some copies."

I stated that was a good idea because I didn't want or need any witnesses. I had already slid my belt from around my waist which Derrick finally noticed. I whipped his behind right there in Brittany's office. I informed him that every time I was summoned to come out to the school from that point forward, I was going to tear his butt up at that school. If his principal was not going to administer the corporal punishment he needed, then his momma certainly would.

After I finished tearing up Derrick's backside, Brittany reappeared. She warned me that the principal, assistant principal, and the receptionist had been debating as to whether or not they needed to intervene on Derrick's behalf. Brittany had told them, "No, sir. He needs that medicine that she is giving him." I believed the biggest problem with the entire public education system was no one disciplined students anymore, which did harm to those students, like Derrick, who needed to be trained how to behave…at home and school. I was doing my part and wished the school would finally do theirs.

I thanked Brittany and informed Derrick that once we arrived home, my daddy would give him round two. I was so annoyed with the school that I was long gone before I remembered that I had forgotten to sign Derrick out. When I left Quitman Elementary, I drove straight to Thomasville, Georgia, and enrolled Derrick into Favor Christian Academy.

Dr. McLean was a top-notch teacher and superb disciplinarian. Derrick tried her the first two days he attended Favor, but after I told him in front of Dr. McLean that she had my permission to use Doughnut as needed. He didn't push the envelope with Dr. McLean any further. Derrick didn't want to take any chances that she may use it. Now that the expectations at school mirrored the expectations at home, his behavior was finally under control. I no longer received any phone calls requiring me to pick Derrick up from school, and he finally started learning something at school. I thanked God for sending Dr. McLean into my life.

I was so impressed with the progress that Derrick was making academically that when my daughters asked if they could attend Favor also, I withdrew them from public school and allowed them to also attend Favor. I believe the academic and behavioral rigor practiced at Favor has influenced the academic successes my girls have achieved today. McKenzie has maintained all A's and one B, all year, and is taking ninth grade courses while in eighth grade. Blanche, who has maintained all

A's for some time, is also in the gifted program and a member of the National Junior Honor Society. Much of their success can be attributed to Favor Christian Academy. Dr. McLean not only helped them to excel academically, but she also instilled in them scholarly habits they will utilize as life long learners. Although they haven't attended Favor in almost three years, I've yet to have to remind my girls to do homework. I don't have to monitor their grades as routinely as I did when they were younger. I don't have to keep up with projects. I don't have to do much to motivate them because the drive to succeed has become an innate part of their psyche.

Derrick, on the other hand, has been trying his best to slowly revert to his old ways. Thankfully, he has some excellent teachers at Cherokee Elementary in Cedartown. They work diligently with me to ensure he maintains his focus.

A NEW JOB OFFER

Unfortunately, I didn't get an opportunity to work toward our goal of increasing MacIntyre's CCRPI score even further. That summer, my superintendent, Sabrina, called me and asked if she could meet with me. She wanted to come to my home to discuss an upcoming opportunity. We set a date and time for her visit.

When she arrived, I was picking blueberries in my backyard and invited her to come pick some berries and talk to me as we completed the task. Sabrina didn't waste any time informing me that she wanted me to become the graduation coach at the high school. Apparently, her husband was resigning from the position to accept a job with an energy company. I thanked her for the offer but stated that I didn't want to leave Mr. Hose because I knew he would need me the upcoming year.

Mr. Hose relied heavily on his instructional coach, counselor, and parent coordinator. Unfortunately, these support staff created great strife between the administration and faculty with their inept communication practices. I believed their manipulation was purposeful and warned him to be careful, since their tactics were souring his relationship with our assistant principal. Most of the time, they blatantly lied about his perception in a matter so their information seemed irrefutable. For example, at the end of the year, the three of them interrupted our sixth-grade level meeting to inform us that it had been decided who would be promoted and retained. They enlightened us that Mr. Hose was making this decision without input from teachers. I did not understand the rationale or fairness of this decision, and I voiced my opinion. They ignored our concerns and started stamping promoted and retained on our report cards.

I excused myself from the meeting and went to Mr. Hose's office. I declared he was making a big mistake by not allowing teachers to have input as to whether their students would be promoted or retained; after all, no one knew the students better than their teachers. He appeared shocked by my warning and informed me that they must have misunderstood him. I was sure they hadn't. All year, the three of them had manipulated situations in the name of Mr. Hose. They reminded me of the Trojan horse in the *Odyssey*. These rejects from the Thomas County school system were causing far too much confusion and chaos in our system.

Mr. Hose agreed with me that it would be impractical for teachers to not have input. He immediately assembled all of us in his conference room to discuss promotion and retention as a group. All of the sixth-grade teachers had input, and everyone was satisfied. Unfortunately, it would be too late before Mr. Hose realized that my premonition about two of those individuals was correct. His counselor and instructional coach's continued manipulation would ultimately bring about his demise in Thomasville City Schools.

Sabrina proceeded to tell me that she was aware of all of the things I had been doing at MacIntyre Park, and she was impressed with 100 percent of my students passing the CRCT test. We had not received our current CCRPI scores, but everyone had come to expect a certain level of achievement. We would not be on the list of failing schools due to our academic gains.

I didn't want to leave Mr. Hose and Mrs. Dawson because we all made a great team; I love challenges, and I wanted to one day become an administrator. The high school's CCRPI score was 64.2 in 2013 and 70.4 in 2014. Even though their score had increased six points, I wanted to see if I could help increase their score more. I knew if I could accomplish this feat, I could move into administration in a few years or so. I knew MacIntyre would be in excellent hands with Mr. Hose and Mrs. Dawson if he would heed my warning about the wolves in sheep clothing masquerading around him. I asked Sabrina to allow me to notify Mr. Hose of my decision to accept this advancement; I wanted him to know I was grateful for the opportunity and support he had given me.

When I informed Mr. Hose about the new job offer he shouted, "Tell her no! You can't leave MacIntyre Park."

I figured that would be his response to my news. I explained to him that I didn't want to leave either. It was rare to find supportive administrators, and I was blessed to have found two. However, I did have aspirations to one day become an administrator, and this assignment would be a perfect opportunity for me to prove my worth to the system. Mr. Hose said that he understood this and wished me the best.

I looked forward to becoming the graduation coach because I knew most of the students in the upcoming Freshman Class. They had graduated from our eighth-grade class at MacIntyre Park. Despite the fact that I often fussed at many of them for disturbing me as they noisily descended the stairs located next to my room, they respected me and were also excited that I was their new graduation coach.

4 POMP AND CIRCUMSTANCES

Although my new principal, Todd, made it known to me that he didn't have any input when it came to me being placed in this new position, he was extremely supportive. Little did he know that I didn't have much input myself, and I honestly was not seeking to come to his school. I think Todd thought I was getting the proverbial "hook up," but unbeknownst to him I did not know Sabrina prior to coming to the system.

Like Sabrina, Todd was born and raised in Thomasville and had matriculated through the Thomasville City School System. He was a good guy, and I admired that. However, he was far too lenient for my taste. I quickly comprehended that some of his teachers took advantage of his generosity. One of the Career, Technical and Agricultural Education (CTAE) teachers made it her business to let me know that there were others who wanted the position that I was given, so there were targets firmly placed on my back. I also realized that the job was far more challenging than I initially thought.

My first task as graduation coach was to host an orientation for our upcoming freshmen. I knew all eyes would be on me to see how well I completed this task, so I deliberately planned every detail. Todd made sure I was well aware of the fact that we had no budget. This didn't bother me because I had already decided the prior year that when I returned to education, I would give my local supplement, whatever it was, back to the system. That was in addition to the already generous amount that I spent on my class and school every year anyway.

For this event, I got creative. I created a pin for my frat brothers, the men of Phi Beta Sigma Fraternity, Inc. and sold them at their centennial conference. My frat brothers' generosity enabled me to serve Chick-fil-A sandwiches to the students and their parents. Todd informed me that the attendance was the highest he had seen in years. At that moment, I promised myself I would be on my best behavior at Thomasville High School because Sabrina was indeed correct; I was perfect for this job.

I had always viewed myself as being a voice for students, particularly those whom others believed to be a problem. This had often caused problems between my coworkers and me. They would become upset with me for not taking what they deemed "their side" of an issue. Whether they were right or wrong, I was supposed to always agree with whatever they said or did, and I couldn't always do that. I can understand the need for teachers to present an undivided front in front of the kids.

It's no secret that when students sense division among their teachers, they will more than likely manipulate the situation to their advantage. It's the same as when they forge their parents against each other to do, or get, whatever benefits them most. Regardless of this, when it comes to students, there should never be sides, only what's in the best interest of the kids being served.

Needless to say, as graduation coach, I felt my most important job was to monitor students' grades. I wanted to remain abreast of their grades so that I could offer support to our students before it was too late to do anything about them failing. To accomplish this goal, I checked every student's grades on a weekly basis. Yes! I pulled the grades of a little over 400 students every week. I told the students up front that if anyone failed two or more classes, they were on MY "probation," which meant they would have to report to me weekly until their grades improved. When they reported, they would be given a progress report for them to take home for a parent's signature. Upon return, I would file all signed progress reports.

Approaching week three, I had to make good on my promise of probation. The students were shocked when they saw that I was taking my new role as *probation officer* very seriously. I was shocked to see how many of my 9th graders were not taking high school seriously at all. For the most part, my seniors were on track and determined to graduate. However, I realized that I had to meet with all of the 9th graders and make them understand the importance of maintaining a high grade point average (GPA). Sadly, several had no clue as to what a GPA was, though it is a common way high schools and colleges measure their students' academic achievement.

It was evident that the importance of having as high a GPA as possible was not stressed at THS as evidenced by only 9 of our 108 seniors having a GPA of 3.3 or higher. I discovered this while compiling a list of seniors who could possibly be eligible for the Bill Gates scholarship. Whereas only 8% of our students met these requirements, 55 of the 57 Scholars Academy students (96%) had a GPA that was 3.3 or higher.

The GPA is a calculated average of the letter grades students earn following a 0 to 4 scale. To calculate a high school GPA, you must first know a little something about "credits" or "units." These terms are often used interchangeably. Each course is given a certain number of credits, this value is basically the same for each course. Although the core courses (math, science, social studies, and English) are typically worth one credit, a few courses are worth only a half (.5) credit, such as physical education, health, American government, and civics. In Georgia, students must earn a minimum of 23 credits to graduate. Each credit is equivalent to the satisfactory completion of one year of coursework.

Here is the breakdown of the mandatory 23-hour equivalency:

English/ Language Arts	4	CTAE and/or Modern Language and/or Fine Arts	3
Mathematics	4	Health	.5
Science	4	Physical Education	.5
Social Studies	3	Electives	4

Next, I will discuss grade points. The points for each grade are usually as follows: A—4 points; B—3 points; C—2 points (if applicable)—1; and F – 0 points earned. To find the total "grade points" for each course, multiply the number of credit hours by the point value assigned for the grade earned. For example, if a student earns an A in a one-credit class, the total grade points earned are 4; however, if the student earns an A in a three-credit class, the total grade points earned are 12.

The GPA is calculated by simply dividing the total points earned by the total number of credits completed.

$$\frac{\text{Total Points Earned}}{\text{Total Credits Attempted}} = \text{Grade Point Average}$$

Table A

Example Student Transcript			
Courses	Credit Hours	Grade	Grade Points
9th Grade Literature	1	A	4
9th Grade Geometry	1	A	4
9th Grade Biology	1	C	2
American Govt.	.5	A	2
3.5 Total Credit Hours Completed			12 Total Grade Points

$$\frac{12 \text{ Points Earned}}{3.5 \text{ Credits Attempted}} = 3.43 \text{ GPA}$$

I wanted the students, especially the 9th graders, to know how to calculate and make decisions that would positively impact their GPA. I explained to them that when they applied to college, the school of their choice would use their cumulative GPA (an ongoing average of all of their semester grades, beginning with their freshman year) to determine their overall performance in school. They couldn't wait until their junior or senior year to become serious about their GPAs because every single class during their high school matriculation would be averaged in. If they performed poorly their freshman and sophomore years, it would be near impossible for them to graduate with an above average GPA. For example, if a student received all D's worth 1 point in ninth and tenth grade and all A's worth 4 points in eleventh and twelfth grade, their cumulative GPA would only be around 2.5. This doesn't meet the minimum GPA required for admission into most colleges.

Many of my seniors wished they had tried harder during their freshman year. Some of their failures from ninth grade still haunted a few of them.

An F can do serious harm to a student's GPA. For instance, if the biology grade in Table A is changed to an F in Table B, observe what happens to the GPA. One F causes a 3.43 GPA to plummet to a mere 2.86. When a student fails a class, there are no grade points earned for the course, but the total credits still count. This is what causes the GPA to decrease when a student fails.

Table B

Example Student Transcript			
Courses	Credit Hours	Grade	Grade Points
9th Grade Literature	1	A	4
9th Grade Geometry	1	A	4
9th Grade Biology	1	F	0
American Govt.	.5	A	2
3.5 Total Credit Hours Completed			10 Total Grade Points

$$\frac{10 \text{ Points Earned}}{3.5 \text{ Credits Attempted}} = 2.86 \text{ GPA}$$

> ## GPA Tips & Tactics
> - Work hard in your freshman and sophomore year to increase your change of admission into AP, IB, honors and accelerated courses-they are your ticket to a higher GPA since they are often given more weight on the GPA scale.
> - While a low GPA won't keep you from getting in college, some four-year colleges do require a 3.0 or higher for admission.
> - Don't slack off once you receive your acceptance letter. Your future college will continue to monitor your grades through the end of your senior year and expect a final transcript.

KNOWING GRADES MATTER

Some teachers often complained that it was our parents' job to ensure their child was passing all of their classes, or the students should be more aware of their learning to ensure they passed their classes; I didn't agree with these assumptions in their entirety. I believed it required a concerted effort from parents, students, and teachers working together to ensure our students succeeded. Rather than point fingers and cast blame, I simply assumed the parents' role if I needed to and encouraged teachers to do the same. Even though some embraced this way of thinking, there were a few who didn't. It was apparent that they just didn't care. For them, teaching was all about receiving a check on the first and having their summers off. That's all I could assume when they didn't even bother to update or input grades into the computer.

Several teachers were not updating their grades promptly in PowerSchool, our student information system that teachers used to input their grades, take attendance, and check student demographics, and review past academic data. In my position, I was given administrative access, which meant I could view all students' grades and all teachers' grade books.

During my mid-semester progress check, I printed out the progress reports for my *probationers*. I noticed several were still failing the same classes. This concerned me for I knew the semester would be ending soon. I soon concluded that their grades were the same as those printed on my prior report, so I decided to go into the teachers' grade book to see what was going on. The students' grades had not changed because their teachers had not updated their grade book in weeks. We were midway the semester, and some teachers still had not been updated their student's grades. To make matters worse, there was one teacher who had not input any grades in the grade book since the semester had begun. I was in utter disbelief, so I took a screenshot of the grade report of a student enrolled in this teacher's class to save for my records.

I approached Todd about this problem and asked if he would address it. I even told him about the teacher who had not entered any grades in their gradebook since the semester had begun. He asked me to compile a list of all of the teachers who were not updating their grades promptly, and give it to him. According to him, the teachers were expected to input at least two to three grades in the system on a weekly basis.

As promised, Todd sent an email to the staff asking them to input their grades promptly. The hell-raisers in the building did as normal and ignored him. They still did not update their grades as requested. It was unfair to the students, who never knew exactly what their actual grades were in the affected classes.

At that point, I decided I needed to empower our students. I went into PowerSchool and assigned every student in our building a PowerSchool login so that they could access their own grades. My goal was to have the students access their grades on a weekly basis. I was pretty certain that once the students noticed their grades were not being input with fidelity, they would help pressure their teachers to input their grades in a timely manner. I knew this would not work without some incentive, so I created bulldog bucks and informed the students that they could be used to purchase candy, Thomasville High paraphernalia, and entry into my Bulldog Bashes which would be held once every nine weeks. All they had to do was print out their progress reports and submit them to me. They could earn up to $1 for each of the following: no tardies, all passing grades, four or more A's, no office referrals, and perfect attendance for a total of $5 a week. I knew I had to purchase all of the incentives with my personal funds, but I didn't care if it was going to make a difference.

Initially, the students were reluctant to participate; it wasn't until I had my first Bulldog Bash that the students became excited. I had purposely purchased a wealth of food for my first bash. We had pizza, buffalo wings, sub sandwiches, doughnuts, cookies, brownies, chips, and almost any treat you can name. The event was a huge success, and it increased participation significantly. More importantly, the students were logging into the system to keep track of their grades, which is what I wanted. We went from zero student logins in Powerschool to hundreds within a matter of days. Some students checked their grades daily. As I anticipated, the pressure from the students seemed to make the teachers finally input their grades in a timelier manner.

I encourage everyone reading this book to request their child's login information for whatever grading program their child's school is using and monitor grades weekly. Print the reports so there is proof as to whether or not grades are being input and/or updated on time within reasonable intervals of time.

5 MOVE ON WHEN READY

After our midterm, I discovered I had several female students enrolled in a Certified Nursing Assistant (CNA) course at our technical college. Unbelievably, most of them were failing the course that I had no idea they were taking. Apparently, their nursing essentials teacher had enrolled them in the course. If one of the students had not approached me about possibly failing the course, I never would have known. Far worse, if any of them failed the course, they would not be able to graduate. I knew I had to intervene.

I asked one of the students for a syllabus so that I could get their teacher's information. I was able to chat with their instructor, Ms. Karen Kelso, and she too was shocked at how poorly the girls were performing. I apologized to her for the girls' performance and promised her that I would speak with them about how essential this class was, especially if they planned to graduate. Thankfully, Ms. Kelso was a gem and kept me abreast of their progress. I loved the fact that she remained firm and did not relax her expectations for these students.

This first course was a medical terminology class that consisted mostly of memorizing medical terms. I was a firm believer that if these students could memorize a Beyoncé song and the most popular raps, then they could memorize the information needed to pass their classes. I called the girls in and made a copy of their study guides. I gave each of them the link to my Quizlet site and uploaded all of the vocabulary terms they needed to learn. I warned them that I would be observing them very closely.

My interaction with the girls uncovered yet another uniquely valuable program I was not familiar with at that time: Move on When Ready (MOWR). It is important to share with you what I learned about this remarkable opportunity for students. I encourage any individual who reads this book to please share this information with any and every high school student or parent you make contact with. Given that I will specifically discuss the program as it pertains to Georgia, those from other states need to seek advice from their local guidance counselor, since many other states are now implementing their own versions of MOWR; or simply perform a google search that includes dual enrollment and the interested state to see what options are out there.

MOWR is Georgia's new dual enrollment program that allows high school students in grades nine through twelve to attend postsecondary institutions (college, university, or technical college). The students can earn college credits while they earn their high school diplomas. The new MOWR law streamlines the existing dual enrollment options (Move on When Ready, Accel, and Hope Grant) into one program with one funding source. The programs were consolidated to make it easier for students to take advantage of the available options to enroll in college while still attending high school.

MOWR covers tuition, mandatory fees, and supplies. According to Georgia's Department of Education website, "The goals of Move on When Ready are to increase college access and completion and prepare students to enter the workforce with the skills they need to succeed." The gadoe.org website lists several benefits for students who participate in MOWR to include:

• Introduce students to college-level coursework.

• Earning college credits while still in high school may enable students to graduate early and/or possibly even earn an associate degree, diploma, or certificate.

• Help students adjust to certain aspects of the college experience (e.g., classes, coursework, instruction, being on a college campus) so the transition from high school to college may be

easier.

• *Students who participate in a dual enrollment program are more likely to go to college and get a college degree.*

• *Students may be able to take classes that are not offered at their high school, especially in subject areas they are interested in for a potential career.*

• *Participating in a dual enrollment program demonstrates a student's ability to handle more difficult coursework which is something college admissions officers may look upon favorably during admissions and recruiting.*

• *Taking college-level classes while still in high school may build confidence and encourage those students who may not be thinking about college to reconsider. (retrieved from www.gadoe.org)*

After I researched the MOWR program, I was appalled to discover that the Thomasville High School students were not being encouraged to participate in this program or any of our Advanced Placement (AP) courses either. Only four THS students were taking AP courses in contrast to the 198 students enrolled in AP courses through the Scholar's Academy. We also had only three students attending our local college/universities, in comparison to 43 students from the Scholar's Academy being enrolled. Only eight THS students were attending our local technical college versus 25 students from the

Scholar's Academy.

I was heartbroken. Here was a program that could help these inner-city students prepare and transition to college easier, and they were not even being encouraged to take advantage of this opportunity. Many THS students claimed they wanted to go to college when they graduated; therefore, it only made sense for them to become dually enrolled. Being in a dual enrollment program would give them an opportunity to experience college life at the state's expense.

These kids could also earn an associate's degree or technical diploma while attending high school if they pushed themselves. For students who would more than likely have to rely on student loans at some point, these free college classes were a godsend that could lessen some of their burdens.

The college experience differs for everyone who attends. It is important that students achieve a certain balance when they enter college. For many of them, it is their first taste of freedom. Students are responsible for their schedules, getting to class, completing assignments, managing their grades, and organizing their priorities to maintain a balance of academic and social interactions. In essence, they are immediately pushed into the responsibilities of adulthood. Succeeding in college is all about finding the perfect balance!

Being in a dual enrollment program provides students, (who are confident about attending college and those who may be considering college) the opportunity to find their *balance* and make any needed adjustments prior to entering the college of their choice. There are far too many students who drop out of college after their first semester or year because they fail to find that perfect balance. When students take college courses while attending high school, they still have a support system around them to assist them in making the needed changes to properly adjust to achieve stability. This will ultimately lead to them being successful in college later on.

ELIGIBILITY

Any student in the ninth, tenth, eleventh, or twelfth grades at an eligible public or private high school or home study program can participate in MOWR. Prior to February 1st of each year marks the deadline for eligible high school or home study programs to give program information and materials, provided by the GADOE, to each eighth grade public and private school student and home study student at the time he or she is developing his/her individual graduation plan. All Georgia students are required to complete a **Student Individual Graduation Plan**. This plan serves as the student's graduation guide during their four years of high school.

To participate in MOWR, the student must be admitted and classified as a dual credit enrollment student by an eligible postsecondary institution (college, university, or technical institution). A dual credit enrollment student must meet the MOWR/dual enrollment admission requirements set forth by the participating college/university they wish to attend. These requirements typically include a minimum grade level or age requirement. To find the requirements for the postsecondary institution of your choice, simply perform a Google search.

A student is eligible for MOWR regardless of the number of credit hours for which he or she is enrolled during a school term, and a student's MOWR eligibility is not limited to a certain number of semesters or quarters over the course of his/her high school or home study enrollment.

My daughters plan to take MOWR courses while they are in high school. Their goal is to graduate with a high school diploma and an associate's degree (two-year degree). The girls want to attend the local technical college during their school year, and my alma mater, Fort Valley State University, during their summer breaks; thus, I performed a Google search to see what their requirements for MOWR were, which I am sure are similar to the qualifications for other college and universities. My girls won't begin attending FVSU until their junior or senior year. They can take courses online or on campus but plan to live in our Fort Valley home during the summer and take their courses on campus.

Fort Valley State University's admission requirements for the dual enrollment program are as follows:

FVSU Dual Enrollment Admission Requirements		
• Student Participation Agreement		
• High school academic GPA of 3.0 or higher		
• Submit an official transcript of secondary credits completed to date and evidence that the student is on tract with college preparatory curriculum.		
• Home study programs within the State of Georgia must operate in accordance with O.C.G.A. §20-2-690(c).		
• Students must also submit ACT, SAT, or Accuplacer test scores that meet the following minimum standards.		
Test	Reading (SAT) English (ACT)	Math
SAT	24	22
ACT	17	17
OR		

Test	Reading	WritePlacer/ English	Algebra
ACCUPLACER	63	4	MATH 1111-79 MATH 1001-67
COMPASS	74	60	47

While attending Cedartown High School, my girls will attend Georgia Northwestern Technical College (GNTC). The technical college allows high school students to take college degree level courses and certificate/diploma level courses. Although students are not required to pay out of pocket for tuition, college fees, or textbooks, some occupational courses have course-related fees that a student may have to cover themselves. These programs include but are not limited to, welding, cosmetology, automotive, etc.

My girls will take college courses at GNTC beginning the second semester of their ninth grade year. Grade level requirements at technical colleges are lower; this is likely due to them offering certificate courses.

Georgia Northwestern Technical College Dual Enrollment Test Score Requirements			
Scores for Certificate and Diploma Level Coursework			
SAT	24 Reading		22 Math
ACT	12 English	13 Reading	17 Math
COMPASS	38 Writing	74 Reading	26 Math 37 Algebra
ACCUPLACER	60 Sentence Skills	55 Reading	34 Arithmetic 41 Elem Algebra
ASSET	38 Writing	39 Reading	35 Numeric 37 Pre-Algebra
Scores for Degree Level Coursework			
SAT	25 Reading		24 Math
ACT	16 English	17 Reading	19 Math
COMPASS	63 Writing	80 Reading	26 Math 40 Algebra
ACCUPLACER	70 Sentence Skills	64 Reading	34 Arithmetic 57 Elem Algebra
ASSET	42 Writing	41 Reading	35 Numeric 44 Pre-Algebra

The technical colleges testing requirements also differ depending on which program the student selects. Technical college is perfect for students who haven't quite decided whether or not they want to pursue a college degree. Students can always start by enrolling into a certificate or diploma program first. This is a viable option for the student who decides that pursuing a four-degree may not be the best choice for them. At least they will have obtained a certificate or diploma that can be used to support their livelihood following high school.

HOW TO APPLY

The first step for enrolling in the dual enrollment program is to meet with the high school counselor to determine eligibility and if the program is right for the student. Attending a postsecondary institution is something that has to be taken seriously. The coursework is rigorous and likely will require an ample amount of study time. Additonally, nearly all courses require a significant amount of reading.

Each person's college experience is different; comparatively, the students must dedicate themselves to the cause and put forth their best effort. My son loved college. Even though he was a mediocre student in high school, he swore college was the best kept secret that everyone need to know.

After eligibility is determined, the student must submit a transcript, completed dual enrollment scholarship application form (must be completed at https://www.gagutures.org/), and immunization records. Please note: A new student participation agreement must be completed each semester before a student can register, and a new dual enrollment scholarship application must be submitted each semester of enrollment. The application also requires the dual enrollment courses to be listed and approved by the high school/home study program and postsecondary institution. The courses must be from the MOWR approved course offerings.

The MOWR program does have term specific application deadlines. The student, high school/home study program or parent, and the post-secondary institution must complete the MOWR application and submit it to the Georgia Student Finance Commission (GSFC) by the following deadlines:

Term	Application Deadline
Fall	October 1
Winter	March 1
Spring	March 1
Summer	May 15

ELIGIBLE INSTITUTIONS

Dual enrollment courses can be taken at public, technical, and private college/universities. Below is a list of eligible institutions as of FY 2018. Any student seeking to attend a private college/university would greatly benefit from dual enrollment because private school's tuitions are far more expensive than state colleges and universities. Being that there are no course limitations for dual enrollment courses, completing as many courses as possible during high school will result in huge financial savings.

FY 2018 ELIGIBLE DUAL ENROLLMENT INSTITUTIONS

Public

Abraham Baldwin Agricultural College	Georgia Highlands College
Albany State University	Georgia Institute of Technology
Armstrong State University	Georgia Southern University
Atlanta Metropolitan State College	Georgia Southwestern State University
Augusta University	Georgia State University
Bainbridge State College	Gordon State College
Clayton State University	Kennesaw State University
College of Coastal Georgia	Middle Georgia State College
Columbus State University	Savannah State University
Dalton State College	South Georgia State College
East Georgia State College	University of Georgia
Fort Valley State University	University of North Georgia
Georgia College & State University	University of West Georgia
Georgia Gwinnett College	Valdosta State University

Technical

Albany Technical College	Lanier Technical College
Athens Technical College	North Georgia Technical College
Atlanta Technical College	Oconee Fall Line Technical College
August Technical College	Ogeechee Technical College
Central Georgia Technical College	Savannah Technical College
Chattahoochee Technical College	South Georgia Technical College
Coastal Pines Technical College	Southeastern Technical College
Columbus Technical College	Southern Crescent Technical College
Georgia Northwestern Technical	Southern Regional Technical

College	College
Georgia Piedmont Technical College	West Georgia Technical College
Gwinnett Technical College	Wiregrass Georgia Technical College

Private	
Andrew College	Oglethorpe University
Berry College	Paine College
Brenau University	Piedmont College
Brewton-Parker College	Point University
Clark Atlanta University	Reinhardt University
DeVry University	Shorter University
Embry-Riddle Aeronautical University	Spellman University
Emmanuel College	Thomas University
Georgia Military College	Toccoa Falls College
Georgia Military College	Truett McConnell University
LaGrange College	Wesleyan College
Mercer University	Young Harris College

BENEFITS

There are many benefits to taking dual enrollment courses. The degree level core classes will transfer to any institution in the University System of Georgia (USG) or Technical College System of Georgia (TCSG). The credits earned count toward high school rigor and HOPE Scholarship rigor requirements. Students who take dual enrollment courses get a 0.5 boost in the HOPE Scholarship GPA calculation upon high school graduation. Please note that this boost does not count toward your high school's GPA calculation. One of the greatest advantages of dual enrollment is the courses taken will not count toward the HOPE Grant or Scholarship credit hour caps. This means that students will have enough HOPE aid to complete their postsecondary education.

Anyone who plans to go to college should take dual enrollment courses. While I only discussed the dual enrollment options in Georgia, as I stated earlier, these options are available in many other states as well.

6 SAT VERSUS ACT

It soon became apparent to me that our students needed more information about college. I had seniors who said they were going to college, but had not taken the SAT or ACT, the main two standardized college entrance exams. These tests were a must have for entrance to most colleges and universities for high school students with less than 30 transferrable hours of credit.

SAT initially stood for *Scholastic Aptitude Test*, which was later changed to *Scholastic Assessment Test*, and now SAT no longer stands for anything officially. ACT started off as the American College Test, but the ACT organization no longer formerly calls it that. It is simply known as the ACT.

Most colleges do not prefer one test over the other.

It basically boils down to whatever the student prefers. Though the tests generally cover the same topics, they differ in that the ACT includes a science section, and the SAT includes one SAT Math Section on which students may not use a calculator.

The best way for students to decide which test is best for them is to take a timed full-length practice test of each type. The Princeton Review offers these FREE practice tests for students to take online via their website. I encourage all college bound students to take advantage of this opportunity by visiting the Princeton Review's website (www.princetonreview.com).

I recommend students start taking the SAT or ACT during the spring of their junior year and/or October of their senior year. The tests are given five times during a school year and once or twice during the summer. Many colleges only see a student's highest score; however, there are some colleges who will examine all testing attempts. Thus, students should take every attempt seriously.

	SAT	ACT
Test Structure	Reading Writing & Language Math Essay (Optional)	English Math Reading Science Reasoning Essay (Optional)
Length	3 hours (without essay) 3 hours, 50 minutes (with essay)	2 hours, 55 minutes (without essay) 3 hours, 40 minutes (with essay)
Reading	5 reading passages	4 reading passages
Science	None	1 science section testing critical thinking skills (not specific science knowledge)
Math	Arithmetic Algebra I & II Trigonometry and Data Analysis	Arithmetic Algebra I & II Geometry and Trigonometry
Calculator Policy	Some math questions don't allow the use of a calculator.	A calculator can be used on all math questions.
Essays	Optional: Essay tests student's comprehension of a source text.	Optional: Essay will test how well a student evaluates and analyzes complex issues.

https://www.princetonreview.com/college/sat-act

The key to performing well on the SAT or ACT is preparation. There are several test prep programs available to help students prepare; the four most popular are Kaplan Test Prep (kaptest.com), The Princeton

Review (princetonreview.com), Khan Academy (khanacademy.org) and ACT(act.org).

	KAPLAN Test Prep	The Princeton Review	KHAN Academy	ACT
The Best	Most Practice Tests	Best One-on-One	Best FREE (SAT only)	Most Engaging (ACT only)
Starting Price	$299	$299	FREE	$39.95
Instruction Time	40-50 hours	38-80 hours	72 lesson (1-10 min. each)	116 hours8
Number of Practice Tests	8	4-5	7	2
Private Tutoring	Yes	Yes	No	No

https://www.reviews.com/act-sat-test-prep-courses/

The best *FREE* SAT test prep program is offered by Khan Academy. Khan Academy partnered with the College Board, the creator of the SAT, for its "Official" SAT prep course which is *FREE*. The site offers review and practice materials, interactive quizzes, video lessons, reference articles, and all seven full-length practice tests written by the College Board.

TRIO PROGRAMS

I had no idea that SAT and ACT fees could be waived. By the time I discovered this, all of our fee waivers had been given out. Why this information was such a secret, I had no idea. Not only had I not been aware of the waivers existence, many of our students were not aware of their existence either.

Once I calmed down, I remembered the partnership I had formed with Mr. Leon Smith and Ms. Vera Clark, Thomasville University's TRIO Program coordinators. I had worked with these two, and their director, Mrs. Melanie Martin when I taught at MacIntyre Park. My students there were enrolled in the university's Talent Search Program. The year prior, Mr. Leon, Ms. Vera and I had taken my sixth grade class to tour Valdosta State University's campus. I figured if these guys took us to visit a college, then surely they may possibly have the waivers that I desperately needed to help my seniors take the SAT and/or ACT.

I know you are probably wondering, "What in the heck are TRIO programs?" I am going to stray for a moment to provide a little information about some of these programs, because I feel the TRIO programs are extremely beneficial for first generation college students and/or those students from disadvantaged backgrounds.

The **Federal TRIO programs** are eight programs (Educational Opportunity Centers, Ronald E. McNair Post-baccalaureate Achievement, Student Support Services, Talent Search, Training Program for Federal TRIO Programs Staff, Upward Bound, Upward Bound Math-Science and Veterans Upward Bound) designed to provide educational opportunity for Americans by helping low-income individuals enter college, graduate and move on to participate more fully in America's economic and social life - regardless of race, ethnic background or economic circumstance. Initially there were just three programs (Upward Bound, Talent Search, and Student Support Services), and so the programs became known as TRIO. Today, the eight TRIO programs serve and assist first-generation college students and individuals with disabilities to progress through the academic pipeline from middle school to post college programs.

Although TRIO programs have been set aside for low income individuals who are first generation college students, the Talent Search program can accept individuals who do not meet these criteria as long as they do not make up more than one third of the program. I encourage middle school, high school, and college students to take advantage of one of the following TRIO programs in their area.

- **Educational Talent Search**: Provides supportive services to $6^{th} - 12^{th}$ grade students to increase the number of youth graduating from high school and entering the college of their choice. This includes adults who are seeking to re-enter the educational process for the GED or for veterans and other adults who seek to enter college.
- **Upward Bound**: Helps high school students increase their likelihood of graduating from high school followed by college completion by administering programs related to academic instruction and cultural and social enrichment activities.

- **Gear Up (Gaining Early Awareness and Readiness for Undergraduate Programs)**: Serves a cohort of students who attend middle and high school, specifically students who are in the eighth, ninth, and tenth grades. The program encourages students to study hard, stay in school, and enter into a postsecondary institution and graduate. This is accomplished via school tutorials, field trips, workshops and in-school activities.

- **Student Support Services**: Assists with the academic development of college students and motivates those students to successfully obtain their college degree and potentially move to graduate level work.

- **Educational Opportunity Centers**: Provides counseling and information on college admissions to qualified adults who want to enter or continue a program of postsecondary education. The program also provides services to improve the financial and economic literacy of participants.

College/University	Program	Office Location	Phone
\multicolumn{4}{c}{TRIO Directory for Georgia as of 2016/2017}
Abraham Baldwin Agricultural College	UB	Tifton	229-391-5150
Alpha Phi Alpha Fraternity, Inc.	ETS	Macon	478-746-4518
Armstrong State University	SSS	Savannah	912-344-3270
Atlanta Metropolitan State College	UB, UB M/S, ETS, SSS	Atlanta Thomaston	404-756-4059
Clark Atlanta University	UB, ETS	Atlanta Lagrange	404-880-8270 404-880-6093 706-884-8376
College of Coastal Georgia	SSS	Brunswick	912-279-5795
Concerted Services, Inc.	ETS	Reidsville Waycross	912-557-6687 912-285-6083
Fort Valley State University	ETS, UB, SSS	Fort Valley	478-825-1817 478-825-6965 478-822-7195
Georgia Southern University	SSS	Statesboro	912-478-2387
Georgia State University	ETS, UB, UB M/S, SSS (Classic & Stem), EOC	Atlanta	404-413-1690
Georgia State at Perimeter College	SSS, UB	Decatur Clarkston	678-891-2790 678-891-3141
Mercer University	SSS, EOC, UB	Macon McDonough	478-301-2686 478-301-2440 478-301-2099

			678-547-6544
Middle Georgia Center for Academic Excellence, Inc.	ETS, UB	Macon	478-745-1675 478-621-5342
Morehouse College	UB, UB M/S, ETS	Atlanta	404-215-2671
Paine College	SSS, UB	Augusta	706-821-8271
Savannah State University	ETS, SSS, UB	Savannah	912-358-3477
Thomas University	ETS	Thomasville	229-227-6929
University of Georgia	ETS, UB	Athens	706-542-1583 706-542-4128
Valdosta State University	ETS	Valdosta	229-33-5463

Test Waivers

Now, let's get back to the waivers.

Mr. Leon and Ms. Vera did indeed have the much needed waivers, and they gave me SAT and ACT waivers to give my seniors.

SAT and ACT waivers are available to low income 11th and 12th grade students in the U.S. or U.S. territories. Students are eligible for fee waivers if they can say "yes" to any of these items:

- Enrolled in or eligible to participate in the National School Lunch Program (NSLP). **This requirement cannot be used if the entire school participates in federal programs such as Community Eligibility. Other criteria or indicators to determine student fee waiver eligibility must be used**;

- Annual family income falls within the Income

Eligibility Guidelines set forth by the USDA Food and Nutrition Service;

Number of Members in Household (including head of household)	Total Annual Income (for preceding calendar year)
1	$22,311
2	$30,044
3	$37,777
4	$45,510
5	$53,243
6	$60,976

- Enrolled in a federal, state, or local program that aids students from low-income families (e.g. Federal TRIO programs such as Upward Bound);
- Family receives public assistance;
- Live in federally subsidized public housing or a foster home, or are homeless; and/or
- A ward of the state or an orphan.

SAT WAIVERS

Students who qualify for SAT waivers can take advantage of the following SAT services for free or at a reduced rate:

- Up to two registrations for the SAT and up to two registrations for the SAT Subject Tests—a total of four fee waivers. One fee waiver card covers one SAT registration or up to three SAT Subject Tests on one test day ($94 maximum value).

- Four additional score reports, which can be ordered at any time during the student's testing timeline ($48 maximum value).

- The Question-and-Answer Service (QAS) or the Student Answer Service (SAS). Students must order the service when registering to get it at no charge ($18 maximum value).

- Coverage of the non-U.S. regional fee for students testing internationally ($53 maximum value).

- **Up to four College Application Fee Waivers.**

- Up to eight CSS/Financial Aid PROFILE® fee waivers to use to apply online for nonfederal financial aid.

  Visit **profileonline.collegeboard.org** for more information.

Starting this year, the 2017-2018 school, SAT fee waivers will no longer have an expiration date. Students may use any remaining fee waiver cards in subsequent years.

ACT WAIVERS

The ACT fee waivers cover the registration fee for either the ACT (no writing) or ACT with writing. Students may use a maximum of TWO separate ACT fee waivers. This fee includes one report to the high school and up to four college choices. Waivers may NOT be used to pay for any additional fees, products, or services;

however, ACT waivers do offer access to Test Prep Tools. Students registering with a fee waiver will also receive free access to ACT® Kaplan Online Prep Live, which includes full access to ACT® Online PrepTM.
ACT fee waivers are valid through August 31 each year.

It is important, whether students use SAT or ACT fee waivers, for students to follow through to the test. When students fail to show up for the test, they not only miss a valuable opportunity; they prevent others from testing at that test center. It is extremely important that fee-waiver-eligible students sit for these tests.

7 COLLEGE NIGHTS

After the episode with the waivers, I decided that I needed to host some *College Nights* to ensure that our college bound students were provided all of the information that they needed for college. Mr. Leon and Ms. Vera were onboard with this idea and offered to assist me with this endeavor. My vision was to have the students receive assistance to complete their college and financial aid applications.

Mr. Hose suggested I also invite his Kappa Alpha Psi Fraternity brothers to volunteer to help us with these nights. He gave me Mr. Marvin Dawson's contact information and told me to call him, which I did. Mr. Dawson was more than happy to assist with our efforts to disseminate information and provide assistance to families in attendance. He assured me that his fraternity brothers and he would support the initiative. I made copies of applications for all colleges students were interested in attending, and the Kappas did come through for us as promised. The Kappa's, Mr. Dawson, Dr. Deshazior-Hill, Mr. Leon, Ms. Vera and I made sure that all college bound students applied for college.

Applying to college has become so much easier. Now students can create a GA Futures account at www.gafutures.org and apply online. I have already created accounts for my daughters, who are in the sixth and eighth grades.

Staff from Bainbridge College assisted me with my financial aid night. Since all students who plan to attend college must complete a Free Application for Federal Student Aid (FAFSA) application if they desire any federal aid, I again had *the crew* come out and assist my students and their parents with this process.

If you would like more information about financial aid, please continue reading this chapter. If not, please go ahead to chapter five: Dr. McCluskey Cares.

FINANCIAL AID

The Free Application for Federal Student Aid (FAFSA) is a form that students (undergraduate and graduate) complete every year to determine their eligibility for Federal Student Aid. A program of the United States Department of Education, Federal Student Aid is the largest provider of student financial aid in the nation. The office of Federal Student Aid provides more than $120 billion in grants, loans, and/or work-study funds for more than 13 million students to attend college or career school. The FAFSA can be completed online and is **FREE.**

Financial aid pays college expenses such as tuition and fees, room and board, books and supplies, transportation and other college-related expenses. FAFSA determines a student's eligibility for: Federal Student Aid (Pell Grants and student loans); State Financial Aid (Hope Scholarship and Grant programs); Institutional Financial Aid (Institutional Scholarships offered by a college); and Private Financial Aid (Private Scholarships provided by businesses or other organizations).

FEDERAL STUDENT AID

Federal student aid includes grants, loans, and work-study. **Grants** are a type of financial aid that **DO NOT have to be repaid**, unless the student withdraws from school and owes a refund. The most common grant that students receive is typically the **Federal Pell Grant**. Pell grants are awarded to undergraduate students who have exceptional financial needs. Only students who have NOT earned a bachelor's or graduate degree are eligible. The amount of Pell Grant changes yearly and depends on the student's financial need, cost of attendance, whether the student is full-time or part-time, and whether the student is attending school for a full academic year or less. Students can receive a Pell grant for a maximum of 12 semesters.

A **Federal Supplemental Educational Opportunity Grant (FSEOG)** is a grant for undergraduate students with exceptional financial need. This grant is awarded to undergraduate students who have exceptional financial need. Only students who have NOT earned a bachelor's or graduate degree are eligible for this grant. Federal Pell Grant recipients receive top priority, and the availability of funds is determined by the individual institution; thus, it is important that students apply early. Please note, not all colleges participate in the FSEOG program.

The TEACH (Teacher Education Assistance for College and Higher Education) Grant is another grant available for undergraduate, post-baccalaureate or graduate students who are or will be taking coursework to become elementary or secondary teachers. Students who receive this grant must agree to teach for a minimum of four years (within eight years of completing their academic program) as a full-time teacher in a high need field (bilingual education and English language acquisition, foreign language, mathematics, reading specialist, science, special education, and any other field that has been identified as high-need by the federal government, a state government, or a local education agency). If students fail to complete their teaching service commitment, their grants will be converted to a Direct Unsubsidized Loan which must be repaid.

Student Loans are borrowed monies for college or career school, and these funds must be repaid. There is a limit on the amount that students can borrow each year and overall. There are federal student loans (funded by the federal government) and private student loans (nonfederal loans made by a lender such as a bank, credit union, state agency, or a school. The differences between federal and private students are listed in the table below.

Federal Student Loans	Private Student Loans
Do not have to be repaid until the student graduates, leave school, or change their enrollment to less than half-time.	Many require payments while the student is still enrolled in school.
Fixed interest rates (the percentage at which interest is calculated on your loan) that are often lower than private loans.	Variable interest rates
Often subsidized, which means the government pays the interest while the student is in school on at least a half-time basis.	Are unsubsidized, which means no one pays the interest on the loan by the student.
No credit check required for most student loans (except for PLUS loans).	Require an established credit record; the cost of a private loan will depend on credit scores and other factors.
No cosigner required in most cases.	May require a cosigner.
Interest may be tax deductible.	Interest may not be tax deductible.
Federal loans can be consolidated into a Direct Consolidation Loan (a loan that combines one or more federal student loans into one new	Private student loans cannot be consolidated into a Direct Loan Consolidation.

loan).	
If a student has trouble repaying the loan, he/she may be able to obtain a forbearance (loan payments are temporarily suspended or reduced due to financial hardships) or deferment (temporary postponement of payment under certain conditions and interest does not accrue on the subsidized portion of certain federal student loans).	Private student loans may not offer forbearance or deferment options.
May be eligible to have some portion of the loan forgiven (cancellation of a student's obligation to repay all or a portion of their student loan) if the student works in public service.	Unlikely that lender will offer a loan forgiveness program.

www.gafutures.org

The federal government provides loans to students and their parents. **Parent loans** require a credit check, but the loans to students do not. The **William D. Ford Federal Direct Loan (Direct Loan) Program** is the largest federal student loan program. There are four major types of federal student loans: **Direct Subsidized Loans, Direct Unsubsidized Loans, Direct PLUS Loans, and the Perkins Loan Program**.

Direct Subsidized Loans are available to undergraduate students with a financial need. The college/university determines the amount the student can borrow, and the amount may not exceed their financial need. The U.S. Department of Education pays the interest on a Direct Subsidized Loan while the student is in school at least half-time, for the first six months after the student leaves school, and during a period of deferment.

Direct Unsubsidized Loans are available to undergraduate and graduate students. Students are not required to demonstrate any type of financial need. The school determines the amount the student can borrow based on the cost of attendance and other financial aid the student may receive. The student is responsible for paying the interest on Unsubsidized loans during all periods.

Direct PLUS Loans are available to graduate or professional students and parents of dependent undergraduate students to help pay for education expenses not covered by other financial aid. These loans are provided by the U.S. Department of Education and require a good credit history or an endorser (cosigner).

Direct Consolidation Loans allow the student to combine all of their eligible federal student loans into a single loan with a single **loan servicer (a company that collects payments and performs other administrative tasks associated with maintaining a student loan on behalf of a lender, or organization that initially made the loan)** and a monthly consolidated payment.

Work study is a work program that allows students to work on campus part-time to earn money to help pay for school. Undergraduate, graduate, and professional students with financial need are eligible to participate in the work study program. It is available to full-time or part-time students.

If at all possible, DO NOT borrow money for college. Student loans are NOT FREE MONEY and will have to be repaid...and can haunt students forever. I advise all students to stay away from student loans, and only borrow money as a last resort. It is also important that anyone who cosigns on a student loan realize that if the student fails to repay the loan, the cosigner will become responsible for making the payments.

STATE FINANCIAL AID

Georgia's HOPE Program provides merit-based scholarships for eligible in-state post secondary institutions in Georgia. Merit-based means these awards are based on a students' academic abilities. There are two merit based scholarships awarded in Georgia: Hope Scholarship and Zell Miller Scholarship.

To be eligible for the Hope Scholarship, students must meet HOPE's U.S. citizenship or eligible non-citizen requirements; be a legal resident of Georgia; be enrolled as a degree-seeking student at a public or private HOPE-eligible college or university in Georgia; be in compliance with selective service registration requirements; graduate from an eligible high school with a minimum 3.0 HOPE GPA (as calculated by GSFC); be in compliance with Georgia Drug-Free Postsecondary Education Act of 1990; and meet specific rigor course requirements. As of May 1, 2017, students must have FOUR full academic credits from courses listed on the RIGOR COURSE LIST (which contains a significant amount of Advanced Placement Courses). English, Mathematics, Science, Social Studies, and Foreign Language are the types of course on the list. It appears that students are able to choose any four courses from the list. Some of the courses that I am going to encourage my daughters to take in order to meet this new requirement are: Spanish II, Spanish III, Spanish IV, Biology II, Chemistry I, and/or Chemistry II. I prefer that they complete their English and Math courses through the dual enrollment program so that they can technically "kill two birds with one stone". According to the policy, transcript credits earned in any Dual Enrollment Science, Mathematics, English, Foreign Language or Social Studies courses substantially similar to ones on the Rigor Course List will be counted towards the Rigor Requirement.

It is important to note that HOPE has a seven-year eligibility limit. Effective Fall term 2015, any student who DID NOT receive a HOPE Scholarship payment prior to Summer term 2011 are eligible to receive the HOPE Scholarship until seven years after the date of their high school graduation, GED test date, home study completion date, or the date of his or her petition to receive a high school diploma, whichever occurred first. The expiration of eligibility date will be June 30th of the seventh academic year following the student's high school graduation, GED test date, home study completion date, or date of petition to receive a high school diploma. This means that if a student qualifies for the HOPE Scholarship, they only have seven years in which to use these benefits. I had no clue that this eligibility limit existed, so I hope this information is beneficial.

The deadline to apply for the HOPE Scholarship is the last day of the school term or a student's withdrawal date, whichever occurs first. Students are recommended to submit their HOPE scholarship applications as early as possible; the earlier they are submitted, the earlier the funds are sent to the school that the student will be attending and credited to their accounts

All HOPE Scholarship recipients must have a grade point average of at lest a 3.0 at the end of every spring term in order to continue their eligibility. The scholarship must be renewed at certain checkpoints: 30 semester (45 quarter) hours; 60 semester (90 quarter) hours; 90 semester (135 quarter) hours. The total cumulative number of credit hours for which you can receive payment from any combination of HOPE Scholarship, Zell Miller Scholarship, HOPE Grant programs is 127 semester hours or 190 quarter hours.

It is detrimental that students maintain a 3.0 GPA.; however, if their GPA falls below a 3.0…all *HOPE* is not lost. They will have an opportunity to regain their HOPE benefits if they have increased their GPA to a 3.0 by the next checkpoint. It is important to note that a student can only reapply for their HOPE benefits one time.

To receive the Zell Miller Scholarship funding, students must meet ALL HOPE Scholarship eligibility and meet one of the following academic requirements:

- *Graduate from an eligible high school program as the valedictorian or the salutatorian;*
- *Graduate with a minimum 3.7 GPA (as calculated by GSFC) combined with a minimum score of 1200 on the math and reading portions of the SAT test test or a minimum composite score of 26 on the ACT test on the ACT test in a single national test administration;*
- *Graduate from an ineligible high school or complete an unaccredited home study program and score in the national composite 93rd percentile or higher on the SAT or ACT prior to completion of high school or home study.*
- *Graduate from an ineligible high school or complete an unaccredited home study program with a minimum composite score of 26 on the ACT or minimum composite score of 1200 on the reading and math sections of the SAT and then earn a minimum 3.3 cumulative postsecondary grade point average after attempting 30 semester or 45 quarter hours of college degree-level coursework. This option allows retroactive payment for the first 30 semester or 45 quarter hours after they are completed. This means the student will receive a refund for those hours completed.*

SCHOLARSHIPS

Scholarships are often called *gift aid* because they are free money for deserving students to help them pay for college...and the funds received do not have to be repaid. There are thousands of scholarships, offered by schools, employers, individuals, private companies, nonprofits, communities, religious groups, and professional and social organizations.

A common misunderstanding about scholarships is that they are only for *smart students* with the highest GPAs. This is not so. There are scholarships available for every type of student seeking a college education. Some scholarships are merit based which means they are awarded based on academic achievement. Others are awarded for a combination of academics and special talents, traits or interests. There are also scholarships based on financial need. Many scholarships are geared toward a particular group of people, such as minorities and women. Scholarships are also available for almost every sport imaginable, from football to gymnastics; and there are even creative scholarships for those students who are artistic (drama, music, art and so on).

One of the most prominent scholarships available for minorities is the Gates Scholarship funded by the Bill and Melinda Gates Foundation. This scholarship is only awarded to African American, American Indian/Alaska Native, Asian & Pacific Island American, and/or Hispanic American. The Gates Scholarship will fund 300 students per year, starting with 2018. This prestigious scholarship is an all-expenses-paid scholarship available to a Pell-eligible, U.S. citizen (national or permanent resident) in good academic standing with a minimum cumulative weighted GPA of 3.3 on a 4.0 scale.

I encourage students to seek as many scholarships as possible. Check with the school's guidance counselor for information on local scholarships. Most local businesses, churches, and civic organizations award scholarships locally to their students. It is imperative that students and parents are proactive and perform scholarship searches on their own as well. Make sure scholarship information and offers received are legitimate. Please note there is never a cost or fee to find scholarships or other financial aid.

There are several websites that can be used to search for scholarships.

Scholarship Search Websites	
gafutures.org	careeronestop.org
supercollege.com	studentscholarships.org
unigo.com	careeronestop.org
fastweb.com	scholarships.com
bigfuture.collegeboard.org	

8 DR. MCCLUSKEY CARES

Things were going fairly smoothly for a while until I received a phone call from Sabrina. She called me out of the blue and asked me to meet her at the basketball game. All she would say over the phone was that it was important, and she needed to see me as soon as possible. I racked my brain to see what she could possibly want to talk to me about but couldn't think of anything. I knew several of the high school's teachers were dipleased with me for calling attention to their failure to enter grades; but other than that, I honestly couldn't think of anything else.

When I arrived at the gym, the superintendent asked me to come upstairs to the girls' locker room so we could talk privately.

"Dr. McCluskey, I received a complaint about you today."

"A complaint?" I asked in disbelief. "What did I do?"

"They claim you committed a FERPA violation."

"Are you freaking kidding me?"

Then she proceeded to tell me that the teachers felt I violated the **Family Educational Rights and Privacy Act (FERPA)** when I called a few students' names over the intercom that morning. These were my students who were on probation. As a condition of my parole, they had to take their parents a copy of their progress report (that I provided them) and have them sign it. During the announcements two days prior, I announced to the entire school that there were still students who owed me my progress reports. I warned them that I would be calling them by name if I didn't receive my progress report within the next 48 hours. Most of the students on my list brought me their progress report the next day. Some even had their parents bring their progress reports to my office.

I explained all of this to Sabrina and also expressed that if these teachers were so concerned, why hadn't they warned me before the 48 hours were up that I could be possibly breaching FERPA. They didn't say a word because they were plotting and planning as to how they could get rid of me as the thorn in their side. I reminded Sabrina that she had selected me for this job because she knew I would do right by our kids; I needed her unwavering support if she expected me to be a success.

Sabrina advised me to watch my back. I informed

her that I would; but first, I wanted to know who had filed this complaint, and I would be writing a response to the complaint as soon as possible. She told me to come to Human Resources the next day, and she would make sure that the information was made available to me.

When I left the basketball game, I was hurt! I couldn't believe how resistant and vindictive some of these teachers were. The great thing that would come from all of this would be finally knowing which teachers I needed to shield myself from. Receiving the list from HR of the people who filed the complaint would provide me with that information.

FERPA is a federal law that is administered by the Family Policy Compliance Office in the United States Department of Education. FERPA gives parents the right to access his or her child's educational records and right to have control over the disclosure of personally identifiable information from the records. These educational records contain information directly related to a student and are maintained by an educational agency or institution; in this case, Thomasville High School. Once the student becomes 18 or attends a postsecondary institution (college, tech, etc.), all of the rights given to the parents under FERPA are transferred to the student.

The one thing that my accusers did not realize was that my calling students' names over the intercom did not constitute a FERPA violation. I didn't disclose any student's grades, courses, or any information from their educational records. Furthermore, the information was obtained through my observations, which is not protected under FERPA. Even more important, FERPA statutes did not allow any third party who has not suffered an alleged violation under FERPA to even file a complaint. This meant unless these teachers convinced one of the student's whose names I called over the intercom to file a complaint, they seriously needed to stop wasting HR and the superintendent's time; time that they could be spending finally teaching their classes and entering grades promptly.

I conferenced with each of the students I had called over the intercom and asked them to write a statement, which I planned to include in my rebuttal to the superintendent. It is important to note that each of these students had brought me their progress reports back after my announcement, with a few of them even grumbling that they had to get off of probation because I just wouldn't let up. As I read the students' statements, I was flabbergasted. Not one student was upset that their name had been called over the intercom. Reading the students responses made me emotional. The majority of the statements were thanking me for caring enough about them and their grades to make them turn in progress reports. Over and over, I saw the words, "you care." Satisfied that I had not hurt any of my students' feelings or made any of them feel embarrassed, I placed every child's letter in a packet and took them and my response to the complaint to the central office. No parents or students chose to file any complaints against me, so the matter was dropped.

When I received a copy of the complaint letter, I wasn't shocked by most of the names that I saw. The relatively small list consisted mostly of CTAE teachers. This group was a tight-knit bunch who, for the most part, stuck together. I had pretty much been fighting with them from day one. Sabrina and Todd had told me that the agriculture teacher wanted my position and was upset because the job was given to me.

The CTAE director also had a major ax to grind with me. She was still upset with me because she felt it was my fault a parent had reduced her to tears during a parent conference we had a few weeks earlier. One of her ninth graders had come to me complaining about her entering wrong grades for him in the computer. He accused her of not liking him. Initially, I thought that maybe he was overreacting, and this was a simple oversight, but it continued to occur. Finally, I told the student to take a picture of all of his graded papers so he would have proof that his grades were being manipulated. When he did this, it was clear that she was entering the wrong grade for him in PowerSchool, and from conversations with her about this student, I realized that the dislike he imagined was not a figment of his imagination. It was real. Ironically, if I had not given the students access to their grades, no one would have been the wiser that grades were being entered incorrectly. Whether this was being done purposely, I honestly didn't know. I do know that this teacher failed 18/28 (64%) of her students first semester and 10/25 (40%) of her students during our second semester.

The nursing essentials teacher was another name I had expected to see on the complaint. I personally believed she didn't like me because I had invaded her territory. I was told that before I arrived at the school, Todd would get her to deal with unruly students. Since my arrival, I had been dealing with the students, mostly the ninth graders I knew quite well. My principal had me, and not her, ride with him to students' houses as needed. It irritated me how she, although obviously not black, behaved like the stereotypes that most people associate with being black. I could hear her coming to my office before I saw her. It irritated me how she would act like the stereotypical *ghetto* person, which I didn't particularly care for since I didn't want our students to equate rolling their necks, snapping fingers, and the use of Ebonics with being a black person. Just because I'm black, it doesn't mean that I'm ghetto; she proved that all ghetto people are not black.

To make matters worse between us, I had responded to an email that she sent to our staff about parking. Everyone was displaced due to a new gym being built, and she wanted special consideration for the teachers who normally parked in the back parking lot. She sent out a mass email to the entire faculty and staff stating:

Good Morning,

I understand that we have all been displaced

regarding the parking lot up front. What I think you do not understand is that there are teachers who park in the back and have done so for years. I find it inconsiderate that WE now have to "hope" that we can park near our building. I'm sorry if this upsets you, but we should be allowed to continue to park where we have for years and not have someone else take our area. We would not TAKE your spots up front.

Being that this individual had been at the high school for years, I was informed that this type response was a norm for her. By this time, I was fed up with the CTAE director and this individual who had been trying her hardest to alienate the staff and me. I responded to the email:

I respectfully disagree.

Webster defines inconsiderate as "thoughtlessly causing hurt or inconvenience to others." This is definitely not the case here!!!

Everyone has been displaced and is trying to make the best of a situation that was thrust upon all of us. Parking should be first come, first served since it has NEVER been assigned to the back and should not be done so now. Those who have parked in the back for years chose to disregard assigned parking spaces in the front to make it more convenient for them.

We are all in this together!!!

Therefore, I wasn't surprised in the least to see her name on the complaint letter.

I was hurt to see the business education teacher's name on the list. I thought that our relationship was a fairly decent one. He was the only CTAE teacher, besides the art teacher, who even spoke to me on a consistent basis. I had even spoken to Sabrina on his behalf about his load, which was stressing him out at the time. I confronted him about his participation while driving back to the high school after retrieving the letter. The individual claimed not to realize that the correspondence was being sent to the central office.

The only other surprise on the list was an English teacher, who I had helped quite a bit that year. I had worked on her behalf to have students removed from her class to make it easier for her to teach. I was so wounded by seeing her name that I called her into my office to talk with her face to face. I let her know that in education, it is important to remain neutral due to the politics involved. I advised that she never knew who may be her next boss. Consequently, it was best to steer clear of other's agendas. I also let her know that depending on the allegation, someone's career could be severely injured, particularly when allegations were reported to the central office. She appeared to be sincerely sorry for what had occurred to me and apologized for her role in the incident.

9 INDEBTED TO ME

I was offered a contract for the 2015-2016 school year and was quite ecstatic. I had accomplished a lot in one year. The class of 2015 was one of the biggest that had graduated from Thomasville High School in a while. In 2014, there were only 116 grads, and there were 153 students in the class of 2015. If I had not fought like a wildcat, several students would not have graduated. There were over 20 students who had not completed their online coursework within the last nine weeks of school. I was livid because I had no idea that these students were even taking an online course. All of the students who I had enrolled in online courses had completed their courses. To ensure that these seniors made it across the finish line, I literally kept the school open. I assembled a team to help me supervise because, with all the accusations that I had endured all year, I didn't want anyone being able to accuse me of any impropriety. I take my reputation very seriously.

Dr. Patricia DeShazior-Hill, an administrator from the Scholar's Academy, and I partnered with our Twenty-first Century After School site manager, Ms. Terrica Stewart, and her staff, Ms. Nikki Sales and Ms. Constance Hudson, to make sure that the students completed their assignments. We allowed students to work after school and even on Saturdays. There were several nights we remained at the school until 10:00 p.m. I was determined that everyone was walking across that stage. I will be forever grateful to the Twenty-first Century Executive Director, Mrs. Lisa Billups, for ensuring that these resources were made available to us.

For once, I was proud of myself. I hadn't stepped on too many toes, and I had made a hell of a difference. Little did I know my world was about to be shattered; this time, I could honestly say, I didn't do a thing.

We had a few days left before our contracts were due when I received a text message from Sabrina.

The text said something to the effect: *I hear you are telling people that [we] are indebted to you for getting my husband a job with your uncle!*

I had to reread the text to verify the words I had just read.

I knew immediately what was going on. After realizing they couldn't touch me professionally because I was doing a wonderful job, my nemesis had decided to manipulate the relationship between Sabrina and me by dragging her family into the fray. It was no secret that our superintendent was extremely protective of her family members, and they were clearly off limits. Her son had taught with me at MacIntyre Park, and her daughter-in-law taught next door at Scott Elementary. I was, and still am, good friends with her sister.

I was mortified and disappointed at the same time. I couldn't believe that Sabrina would even believe such a baseless allegation. Clearly pissed to the highest level of pistivity, I dialed her number to talk to her.

When she answered, I said that I couldn't believe the text I had just read on my phone and demanded to know who had told her such a thing. She replied, "The white teachers at the high school." Bingo. I was indeed correct that my favorite people were playing games. I explained to Sabrina that I had never made such a statement in the first place; and secondly, neither of us realized that her husband had a relationship with my uncle prior to her transferring me. She acknowledged this fact, but I could tell she believed what those teachers had told her. Later, when Sabrina dissolved my position, I was sure she believed what she had been told.

Strangely enough, I blamed her husband for the entire fiasco. I vividly remembered him coming to the school a few days before these allegations emerged. He was having lunch with Todd and me when he blurted out to my principal that he was now working for my uncle. I had given him the side eye and beckoned for him to shut up because I knew that Todd was going to take that admission the wrong way. I had no problems with Todd, but he was notorious for talking too much. I knew he was going to spread that information around the school. Although I can't prove definitively that he did, it's the only way I can think of that the teachers in the building found out about the relationship between Sabrina's husband and my uncle. I know I never told anyone because it was a long time before I became aware of the relationship myself.

That weekend, I drafted my resignation and sent it to her. Even though things had ended as they did, I appreciated her giving me a chance to become a graduation coach. I appreciated everything that she had done for me, and before I engaged in a battle with her, I chose to simply walk away. When one of the board members heard that I resigned, she encouraged me to rescind my resignation, which I did. Sabrina, at that point, decided to dissolve my position and told human resources to tell me to apply for an eighth-grade social studies position at MacIntyre Middle School, the place I had left the year prior.

I didn't have a problem with that because teaching eighth grade meant I would be teaching my sixth-grade students again, which was something I would enjoy. I interviewed with the new principal, Mrs. Tina McBride, who had worked with me at the high school as an assistant principal prior to being promoted mid-year to the new principal of MacIntyre. Whether I would have gotten the job or not, I don't know. I called Mrs. McBride and told her that I decided to move to Cedartown instead. The irony of the situation was the fact that Mr. Hose and Mrs. Dawson were no longer at MacIntyre Park, and now I was no longer at Thomasville High School.

Those individuals I warned Mr. Hose about had staged a coupe, resulting in Mrs. Dawson and him being reassigned by Sabrina in response to baseless allegations – failure to report. It is surreal how baseless allegations caused individuals affected to have to defend themselves against trumped up accusations until they are ultimately proven innocent, which was the case of those two. Thankfully, both were exonerated. But by the time they were, their positions had been filled otherwise.

Yo Gotti, the rapper, has a saying: Men lie, women lie, but numbers don't lie. MacIntyre's CCRPI scores have yet to rise to those obtained by Mr. Hose and Mrs. Dawson in 2014.

MacIntyre Park CCRPI Scores			
2012	60	2015	65.8
2013	64.1	2016	68.2
2014	**77.2**	2017	64.4

CCRPI stands for College and Career Ready Performance Index. It replaced AYP (Adequate Yearly Progress) in 2011 to become Georgia's school accountability tool. AYP was the cornerstone measurement utilized as a result of President Bush's No Child Left Behind Act (NCLB) in 2001, that determined how school districts performed academically primarily based on standardized test results. Georgia was one of the states that chose to opt out of NCLB in 2011 and develop its own accountability measurement instead; thus, CCRPI was derived with the overall goal being to access how well-prepared Georgia students are for college and careers.

CCRPI differs from AYP in that it evaluates all students regardless of their time in the system and includes scores from all subjects (for certain grades only) and not just math/reading. The average CCRPI scores in 2017 were 72.9 (elementary), 73 (middle), and 77 (high school).

When Thomasville High School's 2015 CCRPI scores were released, I was on cloud nine. The numbers didn't lie and proved that I had performed my job during the 2014-2015 school year quite well. Allegedly, there was talk around the central office and high school that THS scores increased because of the recent passing of House Bill 91 and not me. I was amused because I knew that the following year's scores would tell the true story, and they did. The school still has not obtained the numbers reached when I was there during the 2014-2015 school year.

Thomasville High School CCRPI Scores			
2012	62.8	**2015**	**80.4**
2013	64.2	2016	63.8
2014	70.4	2017	68.1

House Bill 91 provided that students no longer had to earn a passing score on the Georgia High School Graduation Test (GHSGT) to earn a high school diploma. The GHSGT test was first administered in 1991 and caused many students to be denied a high school diploma solely because they did not receive a passing score on all parts of the GHSGT.

The good news is that any individual who met all other local and state requirements to graduate but was denied a diploma solely because they did not achieve a passing score on any of the graduation tests and were denied a diploma, can now petition their local school systems to determine their eligibility to receive their high school diploma. Before I left Thomasville, I called several of the former students whose names I found in my files and informed them to come and get their diplomas!

EDUCATION IS VITAL

There should be absolutely no American students dropping out of high school in this day and age. In spite of the inequalities and lack of resources in some schools, there are still no excuses NOT to obtain a high school diploma. The internet has made it possible to enroll in online K-12 programs; the MOWR programs allow students to bypass failing and deficient high schools and many places have choice options that allow students to attend the school of their choice if their home school is failing.

Our youth who drop out of school are unlikely to possess the minimum skills necessary to function in today's complex society and technologically dependent workplaces. High school dropouts are more likely to live in poverty and receive government assistance such as welfare, Section 8, food stamps, and other government subsidies. They are more likely to become involved in crime. About one in every four young black male high school dropout is in jail or juvenile detention compared with one in every 35-young black male high school graduate. Furthermore, dropout statuses have also been linked to poor physical and mental health. More importantly, whenever a youth drops out of school; it significantly impacts our economy as it relates to diminished labor force participation.

We desperately need more taxpayers in this country than tax takers. It's often hard to become a productive member of society without education or training. A high school diploma is typically a minimum requirement for most jobs. College and universities enable students to immediately enter the workforce and greatly enhance their standard of living. According to the GADOE, "College graduates are almost twice as likely as high school graduates to have opportunities for enhanced monetary gain due to opportunities for on the job specialty training and access to technology." College graduates earn more than high school graduates as there is a growing need for more skilled workers, predominately in the Science, Technology, Engineering, and Math (STEM) fields.

A study conducted by Georgetown University found that since 1983, among prime-age workers (ages 23-54):

- Earnings of high school dropouts have fallen by 2 percent;
- Earnings of high school graduates have increased by 13 percent;
- Earnings of people with some college or an Associate's degree have increased by 15 percent;
- Earnings of people with Bachelor's degrees have increased by 34 percent;
- Earnings of people with graduate degrees have increased by 55 percent.

As you can see from the study, it's worth it to obtain, at minimum, a high school diploma. It's also worth it to take a look at Georgia's "Hot" STEM Careers to 2024. These careers are predicted to have the most annual openings over the next several years.

Georgia's "Hot" STEM Careers to 2024
Science, Technology, Engineering and Mathematics

Occupation	Georgia Wages	2014-2024 Annual Openings
Life and Physical Science, Engineering, Mathematics, and Information Technology Occupations		
Civil Engineers	$91,500	280
Computer & Information Systems Managers	$134,700	330
Computer Systems Analysts	$86,800	660
Computer User Support Specialists	$52,700	570
Database Administrators	$85,000	190
Mechanical Engineers	$82,700	230
Operations Research Analysts	$65,500	100
Software Developers, Applications	$94,900	690
Software Developers, Systems Software	$97,000	360
Web Developers	$79,300	140
Health Occupations		
Dental Hygienists	$63,800	200
Dentists, General	$190,100	110
Med & Clinical Laboratory Technologists	$58,800	220
Nurse Practitioners	$95,800	260
Occupational Therapists	$82,200	150
Physical Therapists	$84,300	320
Physician Assistants	$97,000	190
Radiologic Technologists	$52,500	180

Registered Nurses	$64,100	2,980
Respiratory Therapists	$54,300	160
Speech-Language Pathologists	$72,400	140
Social Science Occupations		
Clinical, Counseling & School Psychologists	$77,400	140

    I realize that college may not be the option that everyone chooses. In fact, colleges and universities only comprise an estimated 35 percent of the available postsecondary education and training possibilities. Our youth can still pursue other opportunities besides college, such as military training, apprenticeships, on-the-job training, employer-provided training and specialty schools.

    Whatever options students choose, Georgia lawmakers have enacted legislation to ensure that our students are exposed to career development opportunities beginning in elementary schools and culminating upon graduation.

10 THE WOLVES' DEN

After deciding to finally walk away from Thomasville City, my family and I headed to Northwest Georgia to the retirement home we built in Cedartown. It had been sitting empty during my tenure in Thomasville; thus, it only made sense to return and enjoy our home. My children were accustomed to frequent military transitions, so our move equated to nothing more than another military type move for them. I was so grateful to my husband because he supported my decision to live in Dixie longer than we had initially agreed. During his deployment, I was not supposed to have gotten a job at MacIntyre, and I wasn't supposed to have extended another year to become the high school's graduation coach. All ended well because God sent me in the direction that HE wanted me to go.

I was extremely apprehensive about moving back to

Northwest Georgia. There were so many painful memories for me in Cedartown. We should always hope and pray that things, people, and situations consistently change for the better, and I was hopeful that the district had changed since my departure.

My oldest daughter would be attending the middle school, and my youngest two were zoned for Westside. Of course, I searched the sites to see who their principals and possible teachers were. The middle school now had a black principal. Just as I never thought I would see a black president during my time, I never thought I would see a black principal at the middle school either; so maybe things were different. I still wasn't taking any chances though.

When I saw who the principal of my younger two children's elementary school was, my heart plummeted. It was Leanne, the assistant principal who had made my life a living hell eight years earlier. There was no way on God's green earth that my kids were ever stepping foot in a place where she was in charge. I knew I was placing great confidence in the changes made in Polk School District, but I honestly didn't want to find out if she had been a part of this change. I had forgiven her for the things she had done to me; yet, I was never giving her a chance to potentially hurt my kids.

I called the board's office and asked for a waiver so that my children could attend Cherokee Elementary instead which turns out was the best decision I had ever made. This was confirmed by my next-door neighbor whose grandson was catching hell at Westside, Leanne's school. This kindergartener was being suspended almost weekly. Having been through that vicious cycle myself, with Derrick in kindergarten, I convinced my neighbor to get a waiver and move her grandson to Cherokee as well.

Since her grandson's move to Cherokee, there haven't been any more problems so far this year. When a student switches environment and succeeds, it soon becomes obvious that the student may not necessarily be the problem. Hopefully, my little buddy won't remember his tumultuous year in kindergarten, because Derrick barely remembered his.

I applied for several jobs on teachgeorgia.org, and the calls started immediately. The principal from Rome Middle School called me for an interview first, but I couldn't schedule anything because I had to accompany my husband to Philadelphia for a military-related matter. I now know that was the good Lord intervening because that principal's personality and my personality would have clashed tremendously. I would not have survived a year of teaching for him. I also received a call from two elementary school principals in Rome City. The two schools were polar opposites. I scheduled an interview for both but decided to accept the first offer, which was a position at Anna K. Davie Elementary. I chose to teach at AKD because the student population was primarily all black and Hispanic school and there was only one black certified teacher at the time. I had been in the same predicament before, so I figured whoever this individual was, they would want some company. I know this may seem like a petty reason to accept a job, but I refused to be the only chocolate chip in the cookie again.

Furthermore, I also preferred to work for a male principal. Men tend to be cut and dry and don't typically engage in female drama. My principal, George, was from New Jersey. Immediately, I could tell that he was not from Northwest Georgia. He didn't seem threatened by me in the least. I may be wrong in this assumption, but I think the biggest problem that I had in Northwest Georgia the first time around was not knowing my place. In my opinion, black women in education are most often relegated to the bottom of the totem pole, especially if they are credentialed with a strong personality. This may be why black females are the highest group leaving education in Georgia as well.

I vividly remember Todd, my principal from Thomasville High calling me into his office one day and telling me to inform him of all of my actions and ideas first. He asked me to allow him to present them as his own to the staff. According to him, this would make the faculty and staff do the things that I needed them to do without the constant resistance. I agreed, because at the end of the day, I only wanted what was best for my students. However, deep down, I knew he had to do this because there was this collective group of white women who were not going to do anything that I asked them to do.

George was transferred from East Central Elementary, the school where most of the system's school teachers sent their children. I pulled his CCRPI scores for the years available and noticed he had obtained: 80.8 (2012), 84.7 (2013) and 85.3 (2014) while he was at East Central, which was quite impressive. Although they had dipped the prior year, AKD had also made quite impressive gains over the past three years as well: 47.1 (2012), 71.1 (2013), and 62.2 (2014); I couldn't quite understand why their principal was being replaced.

Curious as to what I was getting myself into with this system, I searched online to see what was going on. I gathered from the newspaper articles that the decision to replace the former principal was announced in the January newspaper, a mere seven months before the school was scheduled to open. The article stated that Berry College and the South Rome Redevelopment Corp, who were both parts of the planning and development of the two centers located at AKD, were in complete shock when the decision was announced.

"Nobody brought this up to any of us," she [Dean McDowell, Berry College] said. "I had faculty asking me if I knew about it when they saw it online. I had no indication he wasn't going to be principal."

The former principal was allowed to complete the school year at the old school; however, I learned, prior to the start of our new school year, he was reassigned to teach history at the high school. I was flabbergasted and heartbroken to hear this. I didn't care what anyone told me beyond that point; I knew that whatever was going on was personal. My administrative position had just been dissolved over a personal issue, so I knew that his demotion being a "personal retaliation" was a realistic possibility.

Mike, who was the superintendent at the time I was hired, had just returned to the system after completing a stint as the assistant state superintendent. Apparently, he had unsuccessfully campaigned to become Georgia's state superintendent and returned to Rome City to become the new superintendent. He was extremely familiar with Rome City because he had spent a major portion of his career being a teacher and administrator in the system. I personally never had any problems with him; however, I don't judge people by how they treat me, I judge them by how they treat others.

The new administrators suggested that the former principal was replaced because he had called the police on several students and parents during his tenure as principal. From what I observed during my two and a half years at AKD, I would have called the police myself, so I never believed this excuse to be a valid one. I honestly believe the former principal's integrity led to his downfall. During my first summer at AKD, I noticed something that didn't sit well with me, so much so that I eventually reported it to Elaina, one of the Rome City Schools Board of Education members. Maintenance guys from the central office were taking desks out of the school. These desks were brand spanking new. Ultimately, we saw two truckloads of desks leave the building. I would estimate at least two to three classroom's worth of desks exited the building prior to any student entering it.

As my coworker and I stood watching this take place, we overheard the workers say that they were taking the items to West End Elementary, the same school the superintendent's kids attended. My coworker made the statement, "This is why they wanted [the former principal] out of the way; they knew he wouldn't have gone along with this!"

When I moved out of my classroom this past September, they had to piecemeal desks from other classrooms to go into my class. I foresee me completing a Freedom of Information Act (FOIA) request for the original invoices to see if the number of desks currently in the school matches the number of desks that were ordered. Who knows what else was ordered in the name of AKD and dispensed elsewhere. Only time will tell.

SEPARATE BUT NOT EQUAL

The lack of resources at AKD commanded my attention upon my arrival. The kids had a brand-new building and brand-new chrome books, but they didn't have any other resources. How purposeful is a Chromebook with no applications? There was no BrainPOP, Study Island, Reading A-Z, IXL—nothing! My two youngest kids had access to all of these programs and more at Cherokee Elementary in Cedartown.

To make matters worse, there were no textbooks or updated consumables for the students to use. Thomasville may have been segregated, but they did at least provide the basics for their black kids. Each kid there had access to student workbooks of some type. For instance, I know all of our sixth-grade social studies classes had a copy of Carole Marsh's Gallopade series, and Test Ready materials could be found throughout MacIntyre Park. Carole Marsh would be furious if she had known Rome City had scanned all of her materials and placed them in a Google drive for teachers to copy. Clearly a major copyright violation.

The few test materials that were in AKD when I arrived were outdated and needed replacing. Here again, parents were being bamboozled with a new building for their kids but a lack of ample resources. New buildings do not help children learn, resources do!

The first thing I did was ask George to purchase BrainPOP and Study Island. I was assured that both would be purchased. When the programs had not surfaced after two months, I approached George to check on the progress of the purchases. I was assured that the programs were coming. By mid-October, I was frustrated. Unlike most teachers, I didn't wait until a few weeks before the test to utilize the Study Island program. I used it from day one to prep my students for the test. This was my secret weapon and the reason that I had obtained a 100 percent pass rate the last year that the

CRCT was given.

Most teachers fail to realize that the reason many students from low socioeconomic backgrounds struggle with standardized tests is because they have not been exposed to the testing format. Students are rarely given tests during the school year that mirror the standardized milestone tests they are given at the end of the year. It's the equivalent of someone asking me to take a test in Spanish. I hold a doctorate from the University of Georgia, but I assure you none of my vast knowledge would help me if I were given a test in Spanish. Depending on the subject, I would probably know the information on the test, but I still would not be able to pass the test because I don't know how to speak, read, or write Spanish. A majority of these students were quite knowledgeable; they simply have not been taught standardized test language, which creates the same barrier that would exist if I had to take a test in Spanish.

By mid-October, I had grown impatient. I contacted Edmentum, the company who sold the program, myself about getting a quote for our school. What perplexed me was the fact that the new principal had transferred from a school with Study Island, so it wasn't as if the program was unfamiliar to him. From my understanding, the program was highly utilized at East Central.

On November 29, the faculty received an email from our principal:

> *I'm excited to have Study Island. Thanks to Betty for setting this up for us. I also received an email*

regarding BrainPOP. This is now available. I will send out an email with the login and password.

Kay has purchased Lyrics2Learn. I hope to have this ready to go by the end of the week. Thanks, Kay. Please check this website out if you get a free moment.

AKD students, after almost five months of school, now had access to Study Island, BrainPOP, Accelerated Reader, and Lyrics2Learn - the latter no one asked for or used with diligence. This is what occurs when teachers are not given any input in decision making.

When we finally got Study Island, most of the teachers were unable to use it because unlike many of the other schools around us, AKD had not been privy to the program before. Betty, the math coach, sent the faculty an email on January 7, informing everyone that the training had been canceled, and in the meantime, an attached Study Island reference sheet could help us. I sent a reply to the faculty and her, letting them know that I would be happy to assist anyone who needed help because I was very familiar with the program and used it every day. Several teachers allowed me to assist them, which was a good thing because the Study Island training didn't occur until January 27th – six months into the school year.

11 WHEN IN ROME

I was beyond frustrated with Anna K. Davie! Not only were these students not being given the proper resources, but they were being groomed for a life of crime. I had never in my life witnessed elementary students being allowed to wreak havoc on a school at will. I often wondered why black youth were becoming so defiant and belligerent when dealing with authority, and it wasn't until I began teaching elementary school that I realized the disrespectful behavior was starting there. Some of our students were being trained from kindergarten to master delinquent behavior. When small kids are allowed to disrespect authority and disregard school rules, they are being trained or *rewired* to become delinquent. Pretty soon, they come to see that type of behavior as being their norm.

Classes equipped with miniature desks, tables, and supplies for youthful bodies, preparing to mold minds in these essential formative years is what I expected to see. I never expected to witness kids as young as kindergarten cursing and hitting their teachers. Barely tall enough to reach the door knob, but being allowed to do whatever they pleased without any consequences. While talking to one of my friends who taught at our sister school, Main Elementary (also predominately black), I was informed that one of their administrators encouraged them not to write a discipline referral for students using profane language because it was "a part of their culture."

I have been black for forty-six years, and I have NEVER used profane language freely in front of any of my elders.

The irony of the entire situation was that many parents did not even know their kids were misbehaving at school in the first place, myself included. Now I understood why my own son's behavior had escalated when he first attended kindergarten upon our return to Georgia. If my high school classmate, who worked at my son's elementary school, had not called me about my own child, I would not have learned about his behavior at school as soon as I had. That behavior was mirrored in many of these kids. Pleased with his new school, my son came home every day and told me that he had a good day at school. I am sure many of our elementary school students were doing the same thing.

I recognized the true problem. Some of these

teachers were afraid of these kids and their parents, which is not such a problem if your administration is a strong one. The earlier conversations that I had with teachers when I first arrived at AKD now made sense. Several teachers had informed me that our parents were "ghetto." They claimed most of them fought all of the time and often posted videos of their misbehavior on social media. Furthermore, the parents supposedly drank and smoked weed all day and didn't have jobs. Unbelievably, one of the special education teachers made a statement to some other teachers and me, expressing that one of his white students deserved some preferential treatment because this child's parents were probably the only parents who worked in our school. I realized then that some of these teachers seriously believed the stereotypes they had been spewing at me. I was also told not to expect our parents to be involved in their child's learning. This commonly used excuse was thought to somehow justify why parents were uninformed of their child's poor academic performance. I was advised not to bother giving homework, because "They won't do it!"

I had come to realize this was mostly bull crap. My administrators and many of these teachers were afraid of our parents based on stereotypes, which were quickly proving to be untrue. Our new teachers were riddled with fear. They floundered as they sought to reason with the information they were given. There was clearly a disconnect between the parents and the teachers, particularly as students advanced through higher grade levels. Our students were exploiting this disconnect to the fullest.

This disconnect bothered me so much that I cornered the superintendent, Mike, one day while he was in the building and explained, "You need an interpreter for your parents and teachers!"

Undeniable confusion covered his expression. As a summary of the facts he was already acutely aware of, I reasoned that this predominately Black and Hispanic student body instructed by all white teachers was disjointed due to the two sides simply not understanding each other. His teachers held stereotypes about the parents that were not true, and the parents didn't particularly trust white teachers for whatever reason. This was a major loophole that the students were exploiting. Unbeknownst to teachers, the vast majority of our parents were authoritarian. They demanded their children conform to strict guidelines. In contrast, the school was permissive, allowing the kids to make major decisions that their parents wouldn't dare allow them to make. We had third graders walking out of their classes on a whim and taking themselves to the office.

I told Mike point blank, he needed more black teachers in the building. The black teachers could help their white counterparts better understand and cope with the black parents and students. The superintendent agreed that the system as a whole needed more black teachers, but he claimed they couldn't find any black teachers. I suggested that he grow them. At my orientation, most of the new teachers had been former students of the system. If the white kids were coming back to teach, why not encourage the black kids to do the same? At least Mike didn't claim the reason they couldn't find black teachers was the absence of a "nightlife!" That statement had been made on more than one occasion. Here again, the stereotypes had crept into play. What educated person would deduce that young black people are incapable of managing a professional and social life?

In all fairness, AKD had some of the best teachers that I had ever worked with during my tenure in education. Their commitment to education could be measured by the numerous days they worked late into the evening. When the administrators made their exit most afternoons by 3:30, no later than 4:00, the teachers would work tirelessly until 7:00 p.m., not to mention reporting earlier than required and returning on weekends. These were hardworking teachers. Unfortunately, in my opinion, they were not culturally competent in regards to knowing and understanding black cultures, specifically when dealing with children from low socioeconomic households. Regrettably, there was a missed opportunity to provide teachers with professional learning on cultural competency.

By October, I was at my wit's end. The new teacher, next door to me, was sinking. Many days my students would say, "Dr. McCluskey, please go next door and help!"

To make matters worse, my administrators seemed to have a sink or swim mentality. They expected these novice teachers, most of them fresh from Berry and Shorter College, to flourish as they entered classrooms filled with children of diverse ethnicities and backgrounds. Different from the classrooms they once learned in and visited while attending college, these new teachers found themselves struggling. If I had not been a veteran teacher and black, I would have struggled myself. It was not fair to these new teachers who had not been prepared or equipped to handle this population. Some of the veterans still couldn't handle it!

I asked my coworker, the only other certified black teacher in the building, Ms. Shannon Roper, if she would be willing to help me with a New Teacher Support Group. Ms. Roper had been teaching for Rome City for almost 20 years, and all of her years had been at the same school, Southeast Elementary. The old Anna K. Davie Elementary, which was located on the South Side of Rome, had merged with Southeast Elementary located on the East Side of Rome. When the decision was made to build the new school, it was relocated back to the South Side and renamed Anna K. Davie, so the kids were still the same.

Although she was reluctant at first, Ms. Roper agreed to help me with the group. She realized things were fairly out of control, and any intervention was better than none at all. I drafted an email and sent it to all of the new teachers:

> *New Teachers,*
>
> *My favorite scripture is, "Do to others as you would have them do to you" (Luke 6:31, NIV). This weekend as I studied my scriptures, I thought about each of you and what I would want others to do for me if I were walking in your "first-year teacher" shoes.*
>
> *My first teaching situation was quite similar to AKD, and the only thing that enabled me to survive the year was my seventh-grade teacher. I was blessed to be teaching on a team with her; She taught me the ropes, and I still quit at the end of the year!!!*
>
> *It took me a year to return to teaching. I missed the challenges, but most importantly, I missed teaching kids. For some kids, we are the only positive thing that they may ever have in their lives, and our influences can often be the change agent that they need.*
>
> *To make a long story short, the purpose of this email is to invite you guys to join a New Teacher Support Group,*
>
> *I have solicited Ms. Roper's help, and she is willing to meet with us once a week. Please respond to this email as to whether or not you are interested, what day of the week is best for you, and exactly what topics you would like covered.*

> *Together we will make it!*
>
> *Sincerely,*
> *Dr. McCluskey*

Four of the five were onboard.

> *Guys,*
>
> *It appears the best date for all is Mondays, which actually works out well because it will give us a week to test our new strategies. We will begin next Monday at 3:15. The meeting shouldn't last longer than 30 minutes, and we will meet in my classroom.*
>
> *Our first topic is: "Strategies to address behavior." Please forward any other topics that you want to be addressed.*
>
> *Together we can make it!!! We can do this!!!*

Ms. Roper and I were excited to be able to share our cultural knowledge with these new teachers to help them become successful at teaching our kids.

Unfortunately, our group was shut down by our administrators before it even had a chance to begin. George and Louise claimed to have already established a group that would assist new teachers. They had a group on paper, but they never met with the new teachers on a consistent basis as they should have. Be mindful, the purpose of our group was to teach the new teachers strategies for formulating relationships with and teaching our black students. Our goal was to help these teachers become more culturally competent. In other words, we wanted to teach them the nuances of "our" culture in regards to how to communicate with our black parents and students. Being of the black race would serve advantageously. Furthermore, new teachers were often afraid of administrators; an informal group would enable them to be far more open with their coworkers, who they saw as equals, rather than their superiors.

I decided to go on the record [in writing] with Mike. He and I had spoken on more than one occasion about the need to assist these new teachers. I emailed him:

> *Mike,*
>
> *I can help or shut up. I am honestly fine either way, but I am going on record to let you know that our new teachers are drowning at AKD and Main! It's not fair to not render aid.*
>
> *Let's face it, finding black teachers will be extremely hard; it's far easier to train the teachers that you have how to deal with black children.*
>
> *V/r*

Mike responded:

> *Dr. McCluskey,*
>
> *I appreciate your willingness to assist our new teachers. We want all our teachers to be*

successful. I believe there is already a structured professional learning program at AKD that encompasses new and veteran teachers. Perhaps you could coordinate with George to incorporate successful strategies into those sessions. All efforts of this type should be coordinated with the building administrators. We can work together to ensure the success of our students and teachers.

Sincerely,
Mike

I responded to Mike and George:

Message received loud and clear. I'll shut up.

I hated to see our new teachers suffer. Nevertheless, I washed my hands of the situation. I still assisted the new teachers, when they needed me, but we had to work together covertly. My administrators had informed them to not accept any assistance from me. Out of sheer desperation, they would still seek my help. Unfortunately, one of our new teachers didn't make it and didn't return after our Thanksgiving break!

FAILURE IS AN OPTION

When we had our first honor roll celebration, I was so upset. I only had one sixth grader, Seantayjah Heard, to make the All A's Honor Roll. Granted there were only forty sixth graders; one out of forty is still unacceptable. We often hear the slogan, "Failure is not an option," but I realized this was not the case at this school or many other schools comprised mostly of children of color. It is my belief that the more school systems tend to segregate, the more children of color will be failed by the system. The academic expectations in too many public schools for children of color are becoming nonexistent. They are simply not expected to succeed.

I was so disappointed with the first celebration that I, once again, decided to give $20 scholarships to the students who made all A's for the semester. Initially, my principal was resistant to the idea, which shocked me. It wasn't as if the money was coming from his pocket. These were my personal funds. All I needed him to do was recognize the kids. My past experience had shown the benefit of recognizing students school-wide in an open platform. Other students would become excited about the reward, focus on their academics, and strive to excel beyond their usual efforts.

Our school was more concerned with rewarding behavior than academics. Each month the administrators recognized students for good behavior. Behaving was something our kids were supposed to do without a reward. They were expected to come to school and behave. George, and/or Louise, our assistant principal, would appear live on our morning TV show once a month and give away a bicycle that was sponsored by State Farm. They would devote great efforts to ensuring parents, the State Farm representatives, and other important stakeholders were present at the school and create a sensational fanfare about a particular child behaving well for the month.

It took three, nine-weeks grading periods to finally wear George down in regards to recognizing the kids publicly for their academic achievements. During the first two nine weeks, I presented the students with their scholarships, and the word slowly spread among the students. What upset me most was George allowing the counselor to present "Be AKD" t-shirts to the students for being Ambitious (A), Kind (K), and Determined (D). It baffled me as to why these students couldn't receive recognition for excelling academically?

> *Dear George,*
>
> *We have 11 High Honor Roll recipients for the third nine weeks. I'm a little disappointed because I really wanted more, but it's more than last time!!!!*
>
> *We really need to publicly present the $20 "scholarships" for receiving high honors. Will you please give the $20 bills at honor's night? You don't have to mention my name. Matthew 6:4 (NIV) tells us to give in secret. "Then your Father, who sees what is done in secret, will reward you." My goal is to motivate our students to achieve more!!!*
>
> *Please think about this :)*

George responded

> *Sure*

I was so excited that our straight "A" students were finally going to be recognized for their academic achievement on AKD TV. When the big moment finally arrived, my students and I excitedly gathered around my smartboard to see the honors be presented. To our dismay, Louise quickly called out the names. We did not even get the opportunity to see the recipients on TV. To make matters worse, Louise did not crack a smile or put any enthusiasm in the process. The entire event lasted less than two minutes, and it was evident that they were just going through the motions just to shut me up. At that point, it finally dawned on me that failure was an option at AKD. Following the unceremonious display, I gave the students their money directly. I refused to fight the administration any longer to give my money away. It would be sheer stupidity on my part to continue doing so.

I refused to let others lack of motivation, as it pertained to academic excellence, discourage my own. Our sixth graders would be graduating that year, and my goal was to have them graduate wearing caps and gowns. I was alarmed to discover that some of our former students had dropped out in the eighth grade. I knew there was an alarming number of our parents who didn't have a high school diploma, but I didn't realize kids were dropping out at the middle school level until my students shared the information with me when we discussed our upcoming graduation. They listed people they personally knew who had dropped out from Rome Middle School in the eighth grade. From my days as graduation coach, I knew that the graduation rate was calculated from ninth through twelfth grades; therefore, this system probably didn't discourage eighth-grade dropouts. It helped their graduation rates.

About a month before graduation, George emailed me:

> *I heard a lot of sixth-grade students talking about caps and gowns this morning. I don't know where that started, or how it got started, but go ahead and tell them that won't be happening. We don't do that for kindergarten or sixth-grade programs. We moved away from that over five years ago.*

I had excited the children about graduating and offered to purchase their caps and gowns with my personal funds. I was beginning to wonder why my proposals were disregarded so strongly when I desired to initiate programs to motivate our students. There was always resistance. I was perplexed and disappointed, as usual, and so were the kids when I told them that they couldn't wear caps and gowns.

To further irritate me, George failed to mention the part where the kids would possibly be dancing at graduation. Apparently, the year before, the graduating class had performed the Whip Nae Nae at graduation.

I was personally offended. Graduation had always been a sacred event for me. I was number fourteen in my family to graduate from Fort Valley State University, and now the count exceeds forty graduates. This was not a dancing event. Dancing typically occurred at the after party, which was held after graduation.

Of course, I emailed my principal:

George,

If any "ghetto" music is played after our graduation tonight or dancing takes place, I promise you I will address our board of education to create a policy banning this foolishness. It offends me! These kids may be from the "hood," but they need to be taught the norms of society.

Did Alabama dance at their graduation? I know we did not at Georgia!
I know the consensus is that it's only an elementary school graduation; but for some, it may be their only graduation, and this occasion needs to remain solemn and sacred. Society is becoming morally corrupt because we sit back and allow foolish things to occur, which makes them seem normal.

Dancing and playing ghetto music at graduation is not normal, and I do not wish to be a part of this buffoonery. It's embarrassing to me because I know the response that this music will generate from the kids and the crowd.

V/r

Initially, the kids were upset, but after I explained the importance of graduation, they were fine. I promised them that they could dance as much as they wanted on the last day of school. To ensure that George did not allow the kids to sneak and get their dance on, I emailed him again:

George,

I just ran the "dancing" and "ghetto" music by Elaina, and she fully agrees with me. Her exact words were, "Graduation is a rite of passage, and these kids need to understand that. They can dance on Friday in the gym all they want if that's what they desire!" Educated blacks do not support this foolishness. Trying to save you some embarrassment!

I'm happy to say that there was no music and dancing during graduation that year or last year!

THE VALUE OF EDUCATION

Many people can't understand why I am so passionate about education. My passion comes from my family. I was taught the value of education at an early age. When I was five years old, I knew that I would be attending Fort Valley State University in Fort Valley, Georgia, an HBCU (Historically Black College and University) founded in 1895, in Fort Valley, Georgia.

Amazingly, during my tenure as graduation coach, many of my students had no clue what an HBCU was. **HBCUs** are colleges and universities that were established before the Civil Rights Act of 1964 with the intention of primarily serving black students. This was mainly because during segregation, the majority of predominantly white colleges and universities disqualified blacks from enrolling. Most HBCUs were established in the South, after the Civil War, with the assistance of northern United States religious missionary organizations. During the 1930s, there were 121 public and private HBCUs across the country, but that number has decreased to approximately 101. Although HBCUs were originally founded to educate blacks, their diversity is steadily increasing. Others (white, Hispanic, Asian or Pacific Islander, or Native American) now make up 25% of their total enrollment.

Why did I want to attend Fort Valley State?

I wanted to continue the legacy that my grandparents, Ulysses, Sr., and Johnnie "MuDear" Marable, started in 1964 when they entrusted Fort Valley State College with their first daughter. From that year until 1985, my aunts and uncles continually represented our family at Fort Valley State College, which later became known as Fort Valley State University (FVSU).

After my aunt, Ronda Marable-Carson, graduated in 1985, there was a gap in my family's enrollment until my twin, Marion, our cousin, Billy Adams, Jr. and I entered the college in 1990. Since then, our family has maintained a constant presence on the FVSU campus. Twenty-nine members of my family have graduated from FVSU, and three members of our third generation of attendees are attending the college now.

My grandmother often asks, "Who would have thought a man with a seventh-grade education would have sense enough to send all ten of his kids to college and pay for all of their tuitions cash?"

My grandfather knew the value of education and instilled this knowledge in all ten of his children. He wanted an education so badly that he attended the seventh grade twice. When my grandmother first told me this story, I advised her that she may not want to continue telling people my grandfather was retained.

She quickly corrected me, "Your grandfather was a very smart man! He asked to go through the seventh grade again because there was no high school close enough for him to attend."

Then she explained how blessed she was that our community, Simmon Hill, had their own high school. But my grandfather's rural area did not. His sisters who attended high school had to live with other people to maintain their enrollment since there were no buses for black children back then. My grandmother was able to complete high school and even attended Albany State College in Albany, Georgia for one year. She couldn't graduate because of financial constraints. When the opportunity arose for her to continue her education after marrying my grandfather, my grandmother's unselfish desire to raise her children outweighed her longing for a degree. She chose instead to ensure that we all received our education and still, at the age of 93, never misses a graduation.

My grandparents may not have been able to achieve their educational goals; however, they made sure their children were able to accomplish what they couldn't and beyond. My mom, Linda Gosier, and four of her siblings decided to become teachers; three of her brothers became dentists, and two of her sisters became nurses and then businesswomen.

My grandfather never stopped educating himself. I can remember, when I was a little girl, finding one of my grammar books in my grandfather's portfolio, where he kept his Bible. Apparently, he had been teaching himself grammar. This self-taught Southern gentleman was an extremely successful farmer, who hired many in my community. By the time he died in 2008, he still owned over 600 acres of land in my hometown of Dixie, Georgia.

I share this information about my family to prove that cycles can be broken through education. My grandparents invested in their children's education, and their investments have paid off exponentially. Parents need to think of their children's education as an investment. Investing early and continuously will reap great benefits later in life.

12 THE DIGITAL LEARNING LAB

At the end of the school year, I asked George if I could please teach fourth grade the next year. I confirmed that I specifically wanted to teach the fourth-grade boys. Our third graders, who would be fourth graders the next year, had been ridiculous the entire school year. Their behavior had been horrible; it seemed as if their teachers checked out before Christmas, and these were all veteran teachers. I was absolutely 100 percent certain that many of our third-grade boys had been robbed of a year's worth of education. Because of my experiences with my son, Derrick, I sincerely wanted to help these black boys recoup the learning they had missed. I didn't want them to become frustrated and give up on education.

People want to pretend that the school to prison pipeline is not real, but I assure you it is. I have witnessed it grow stronger over the past nineteen years.

George informed me that I would be teaching fourth grade, but he also wanted me to teach fifth and sixth graders as well.

Huh?

According to George, he wanted me to teach a remedial class to help remediate students. I was perfect for the job because I was the only teacher in the building who was certified to teach every fourth, fifth, and sixth grade subject areas. He assigned me 13 names I didn't recognize, so I decided to ask my coworker about these students who had been assigned to me. When she looked at the list, she said, "I don't think you are teaching a remediation class; I think you are teaching a behavior class. These are the kids who lived in his office this year!"

"You think so?" I asked.

"Yes!" my coworker replied. "He's probably sick of those kids being in his office all day. He can't get anything done for babysitting."

My coworker was correct. George and Louise did have to do entirely too much babysitting, but it was indirectly their fault. If the two of them had made office visits seem as bad as death itself during the first weeks of school, the students wouldn't have become comfortable enough to walk out of their teachers' classes and take themselves to the office.

What school possibly has rules so relaxed as this?

Instead of being met with fear, they had been met with iPads and coloring sheets to occupy their time, which greatly upset the teachers.

On the flip side, teachers needed to understand that every time a child was sent to the office, a little more of their power, as the boss of their classrooms, left out the door with the child. That's why I never sent kids to the office. On the rare occasion I needed to isolate a student, I would send them to Ms. Roper's room instead. They hated to go in her direction. What irritated me more was the kids knowing exactly whose classes they could and could not walk out of. The entire situation was a vicious if/then cycle that ultimately fell back on the administration. If they had simply put the fear of God in our students about coming to the office, classroom management would not have been as great a feat as it was. The teacher simply saying, "I am going to send you to the office," would have resonated with the student as punishment and should have shut everything in that classroom down. It did when I attended elementary school.

At my elementary school, Simmon Hill Elementary in Dixie, Georgia, my principal was Mrs. Gracie Jefferson. She was kind, nurturing, and caring, but she was a force to be reckoned with any given day of the week - at least in my eyes she was. I was one of those kids who was super smart, but I was also that super aggravating child. I had a habit of completing my work fast and then spending the rest of my time enticing those around me to get off task. Talking too much was my vice, and it often landed me in hot water. At the mere insinuation of being sent to Mrs. Jefferson's office, I clicked my off button. Although she had a paddle and would use it, Mrs. Jefferson never had to lay a finger on me because I never made it to her office and not many other students in our school did either. It was a place you wanted to visit only when running errands for the teacher, buying school supplies, or just stopping by to say hello.

One of the paraprofessionals confirmed a few days later what we all had suspected about my class—I was indeed teaching the behavior class. Apparently, during their meeting with my principal, the paraprofessionals informed him that he needed to do something about discipline in the upper grades. He told them that he had created a special class to take care of the problem.

"I think you are teaching the special class," this paraprofessional enlightened me.

I had already pretty much figured this out, but I was cool with this because I knew I was about to be presented with one of my biggest challenges yet. I only had one stipulation for my principal. I wanted to select three good students to be placed in the class. I felt the students needed to see some semblance of good behavior. George agreed to this stipulation, and the Digital Learning Lab (DLL) was born!

THE LAST STRAW

MyON is a digital book library that provides students unlimited access to a broad collection of textbooks. The books in the program match each student's interests, grade level, and Lexile reading level. MyON was, as they say, the straw that broke the well-known camel's back. After watching my kids work on myON at home, I was convinced that this program would be perfect for the DLL and AKD as a whole.

A **Lexile Level** is a popular method schools use to measure a student's reading ability, and it helps to measure and forecast a reader's growth. Many educators feel that Lexile Levels measure reading ability better than grade-equivalent scores. Though some may try to directly compare a specific Lexile Level and a specific grade, I prefer to use grade level bands which provide a range students should be reading within. The typical Lexile range I am about to share is the middle 50th percentile of reader Lexile Levels for each grade. This means that 25 percent of students had Lexile Levels below the lower number, and 25 percent of students had Lexile Levels above the higher number. Please note, these ranges are not a standard that students are expected to reach; these measures simply compare the Lexile Levels for students in the same grade.

Scholastic Reading Inventory
SRI Lexile Levels for Grade Level Performance

	Below Grade Level	At Grade Level	Above Grade Level	College/Career Ready Expectations
1	99 and Below	100-299	300 and Above	N/A
2	299 and Below	300-499	500 and Above	450-790
3	499 and Below	500-599	600 and Above	450-790
4	599 and Below	600-699	700 and Above	770-980
5	699 and Below	700-799	800 and Above	770-980
6	799 and Below	800-849	850 and Above	955-1155
7	849 and Below	850-899	900 and Above	955-1155
8	899 and Below	900-999	1000 and Above	955-1155
9	999 and Below	1000-1024	1025 and Above	1080-1305
10	1024 and Below	1025-1049	1050 and Above	1080-1305
11	1049 and Below	1050-1300	1301 and Above	1215-1355

There are two ways that a student receives his/her Lexile Level. They can take the school administered Scholastic Reading Inventory (SRI) test, or they can take a standardized reading test (Georgia Milestone) that converts the student's results to a Lexile measure. The higher the Lexile Level, the higher the student's reading level. The lowest Lexile is 5L, and anything below this is assessed as BR or Beginning Reader. The highest Lexile Level is 2,000L.

Student Lexile Levels are important in that they impact the school's CCRPI (College and Career Ready Performance Index) scores. The scores take into account the percentage of students who achieve a Lexile Level equal to or greater than a certain score on the English/Language Arts Milestone Test for elementary and middle school students and the Georgia Milestones American Literature End of Course Test (EOCT) for high school students. The minimum scores that students need to make are as follows:

Grade 3	650	ELA Milestone
Grade 5	850	ELA Milestone
Grade 8	1050	ELA Milestone
High School	1275	American Lit EOCT

I was intrigued by myON because it was making my daughter, Blanche, a beast of a reader. She was in a heated competition with two other students in her class, and she was determined she was going to win. Not only was she motivated, but whereas my students had to wait every nine weeks to see whether or not their Lexile Level had risen or decreased; Blanche was able to see her results each time she took a myON test. She read more and set personal goals; this increased her motivation and

Lexile simultaneously. I was convinced that myON could also motivate my students. I have found over the years that frequent feedback is one of the best motivators for my students, especially those who are least motivated. This was one of the reasons that I fought the Thomasville High School teachers so hard to frequently update their grades rather than wait weeks to do so.

Excited about myON, I asked my principal if we could get this program. I explained how the program could motivate the kids to take a greater interest in their Lexile Levels and could lead to Lexile Level increases. I particularly favored the idea of giving students autonomy to manage and impact their own data. Let's face it, if a student cannot read, how can he/she possibly be successful in school?

When George told me that we had no money in our budget, I was speechless. We were a Title 1 school, which meant the federal government gave us money each year for this purpose. I was thinking, "Surely this man just misspoke! If we had no money, how had it been allocated?" I wanted to know.

Being the inquisitive person I am, I asked my principal for a copy of our Title 1 budget. **Title 1, Part A of the Elementary and Secondary Education Act, as amended (ESEA)** provides financial assistance to schools that have a high number or percentage of children from low-income families to help these students become successful academically. Schools are supposed to use these Title 1 funds to help their low-achieving students meet the state standards in core academic subjects. Although there are strict rules as to how Title 1 funds can be spent, there are a multitude of resources that can be purchased with Title 1 money, especially instructional materials. Even the Title 1 website states, *Funds support extra instruction in reading and mathematics.* I was trying to provide *extra instruction in reading,* so there was no reason for my request not to be honored.

I wanted to review the spending which had depleted this account.

After a few emails back and forth, I finally received the budget from the Title 1 Director.

I was highly upset! Extremely!

I also saw why the Title 1 budget had been darn near top secret.

AKD EXPENDITURES FY16 TO DATE OF JULY 12, 2016	
This includes School Allocation FY16, Parent Involvement FY16, and Carryover from FY15	
PAYROLL FOR JULY-AUGUST WILL BE OUT OF FY16 BUDGET	
SALARIES- TEACHER/PARA/AFTERSCHOOL	119219.52
CONTRACT AFTERSCHOOL	575.00
WORKERS COMPENSATION	404.95
TRS SUMMARY	16597.55
FICA	8372.99
DENTAL/VISION	770.81
ST. HEALTH INS.	27030.35

KELLY SERVICES – SUBS FOR PARA/INTERVENTIONIST	8898.93
OFFICE DEPOT INC. – SUPPLIES	9664.68
OFFICE DEPOT INC. – SUPPLIES	332.87
OFFICE DEPOT INC. – SUPPLIES	25527.83
OFFICE DEPOT INC. – SUPPLIES	979.77
OFFICE DEPOT INC. – SUPPLIES	244.29
EAI EDUCATION – SUPPLIES	628.84
COMMITTEE FOR CHILDREN – SOC STUD KITS	7441.00
NASCO -SUPPLIES	562.24
EDMENTUM-STUDY ISLAND	1732.50
LYRICS2LEARN-SUBSCRIPTION	1500.00
HIGH INTEREST PUBLISHING – BOOKS	624.59
SCHOLASTIC INC-BOOKS	182.64
SCHOLASTIC INC-BOOKS	921.13
TOTAL	232212.43

Here we were with little to no resources and Office Depot had been paid $36,749.44 for office supplies. I still did not have a classroom set of calculators; Office Depot sells those. As unfortunate as it sounds, I remembered teachers receiving their supplies at the end of the school year. I was shocked that the school didn't store the material and distribute them as needed. All of the other Title I schools where I worked in the past had operated in this manner. Teachers would have to fill out a form to request their supplies, and the bookkeeper or secretary would distribute the items to them.

I was concerned because we had several teachers

leaving, and I was pretty certain that those supplies were probably going to leave with them. No one asked for any of my supplies when I left; however, I knew those supplies were for our kids, so I gave some to Mrs. Roper and left those that remained in the cabinets of my classroom. I wonder how many of the other departing teachers had left their portion of the $36K worth of supplies behind. I seriously doubted many did.

To make matters far worse, $172, 971.12 of our Title 1 funds were spent on the salaries of our two academic coaches. Literally, 74.5 percent of our entire Title 1 budget was spent on the salaries of two personnel who, in my opinion, did not do enough for our students to earn two- thirds of the money allocated to improve our students' academic success. Our coaches acted more like administrators than instructional coaches.

Elementary teachers are certified in all subjects; thus, why is there a need for a math and literacy coach at an elementary school anyway? I would prefer to have zero coaches, but since the system swears they cannot live without them, isn't one instructional coach sufficient? Then our school could purchase myON, which was only $6,950 for the entire school year! Furthermore, they could also spend the $12,564 needed to purchase *Curriculum Associate's CARS & STARS* book collections for all of our students in first through sixth grades.

CARS (Comprehensive Assessment of Reading Strategies) & *STARS* (Strategies to Achieve Reading

Success) and *CAMS* (Comprehensive Assessment of Math Strategies) & *STAMS* (Strategies to Achieve Math Success) are book collections that improve students' reading comprehension and math skills. These books diagnose the students' weaknesses and enable teachers to provide direct instruction to meet their student's needs. What I love best about the program is its rigor. The collections' assessments mirror the Georgia Milestone in regards to how the questions are formulated. Often our students will know the information but not know or understand what is being asked of them because they don't understand standardized testing language. *CARS/STARS* and *CAMS/STAMS* help students to bridge this gap in knowledge. When I achieved my 100 percent pass rate in reading at MacIntyre Park, this was the program that I used in addition to Study Island that year, and I have used it every year since.

The Digital Learning Lab was almost a non-digital project. George honestly didn't have money for our digital programming - too bad we couldn't get a refund from Office Depot for the $36K the school had spent on supplies. I declared there was no way I was teaching three different grade levels, three different subjects, with no computer programs. These kids were not going to be "dumped" in my class for me to babysit. I didn't get paid to babysit; I was paid to teach. I must give George credit. He didn't give up; he kept pushing someone somewhere until he acquired a literacy program for my students and some consumable books for them as well. It wasn't everything we needed, but it was a great start.

INSTRUCTIONAL WHAT?

When I learned that the two instructional coaches, Betty and Kay, were earning practically all of our Title I money, I was determined they needed to work for it. If they were being paid to help our children, then that is what I expected them to do. I didn't realize how much these two individuals were not doing for our students until a teacher who had worked with them and George two years prior at East Central (EC) complained about the discrepancy between their efforts at AKD versus EC. According to this teacher, the academic coaches had assessed the EC students and then placed those who needed academic support into small groups they worked with frequently. She couldn't understand why they had come to AKD and not worked with our kids.

This information puzzled me because our students needed an enormous amount of support, so much so that everybody in our building needed to assist. Ironically, the two main people who were considered the "specialists" were doing the least, in my opinion, for the students. I sent our chief executive officer, Debbie, an email to find out exactly what the duties and responsibilities of our academic coaches were:

Debbie,

Exactly what are the duties and responsibilities of

the academic coaches? I am interested in addressing the board of education about the possibility of us having only one per school. This would enable us to use the additional funds for much needed teaching resources, especially consumables.

I would like clarification of their current duties because, from my current viewpoint, they are being used in more of an administrative capacity. In my former system, we only had one coach. We heavily utilized our Title 1 funds for consumables, such as the Marsh books that we currently have to copy; Test Ready Prep Books; Curriculum Associate Resources; Multiple sets of Scholastic Books, etc. We do not have multiple copies of these resources at this time. Teachers only have Language Arts Coach books; which students must use in class only.

Our test scores are evidence that this current coaching model is ineffective. We are wasting almost $200K for coaches who are not making a major impact. The last year they gave the CRCT, I had a 100 percent pass rate in reading. I attribute most of my success to the Curriculum Associates consumables that I used. Last year, my test scores were not what I liked, but they were the highest in this building. Here again, my success can be attributed to the resources that I purchased: USA Test Prep, Test Ready, and Coach books.

With this new referendum looming, it's imperative that we improve significantly, especially at NH,

Main, and AKD. My goal is to be part of a viable solution.

Thanks!

Of course, I did not receive a response to my email from the CEO; nonetheless, the coaches who had not done anything the year prior, finally started pulling students from classes and working with them on their deficiencies. I still couldn't understand why there had been such a delay in them pulling our students for small group instruction in the first place since we had the same two academic coaches and the principal who were once at East Central. The only logical conclusion that I could draw from this was that the faces of the students and their parents were darker which led to different expectations from our administrators and our academic coaches. Why did the level of effort change when they transitioned from a predominately white school to a predominately black school where clearly their help and support were needed?

13 ON A MISSION

Even though George assigned the students to my class, my students never knew he was the real reason they were there. At the end of the prior school year, I met with each of them and told them that I had selected them to be in my class. I told them something to the effect:

> *I am tired of people thinking that you guys are so-called 'bad kids!" I know that you all are not the problem. People just don't understand you. Some of these teachers don't understand you. That's why I begged [my principal] to let me teach you guys because I want to prove to them that you all can behave and learn. Can I count on you guys to help me out? Can you guys have my back?*

Then, I gave them an application and told them I had a waiting list in case they did not want to participate. I knew the thought of someone else probably taking their place would encourage them to want to participate. To further cement this deal, I informed the students that I would be turning my room into a café, just for them. I was well aware of the fact that some kids would probably try to tease my students about being in my class, so what better way to keep taunts at bay than to create a classroom that every student wished they could be in also.

I decided to go all the way out with the café theme. I purchased bistro tables and restaurant booths for my classroom. Fortunately, my friend, Michael Newcomb, is the owner of the Badcock store in Fort Valley, Georgia. We had been good friends since he started supplying my furniture addiction in 1992. Mike was my dealer. When I explained to him that I wanted to turn my room into a café, he was on board. When the tables went on sale, he called me to let me know. My other friend, Jarvis McCrary, came all the way from Fort Valley to AKD and put them together for me. These guys were my heroes. We also had a lounge area which had a loveseat and two armchairs.

To make the room as authentic as possible, I bought us an OPEN sign, which I turned on during the day. The students were shocked, to say the least, and as I predicted. Everyone wanted to be in our classroom, and it was no longer seen as the behavior class.

THE GAPS

The first thing I noticed about my new class was the significant gaps in knowledge that most of my students displayed. It was quite evident that their behavior had seriously affected their learning. Basic skills in math were almost nonexistent, and I quickly realized that reading was going to be a struggle. The foundation was not there; this troubled me.

Elementary school is the foundation of a student's education. If they do not master basic skills during their formative years, they are being set up for failure. I believe we should focus solely on math and reading in grades K-2. The science and social studies could be introduced through the student's reading assignments in those grades.

A house cannot be built on a shaky foundation. Why would we think that an educational career could be built upon one? It is extremely important that parents make sure their child does not leave kindergarten without the basic skills. Kindergarten is the grade that all parents should not have a problem helping their child with their work; there is absolutely no reason that these kids should not know their letter sounds or master their sight words. I would prefer to retain a child in kindergarten rather than do so in any other grade because kindergarten is the most important grade that needs to be mastered to set up a solid foundation. Most importantly, retention in kindergarten is not an embarrassment to the child because they are too young to care about peer pressure.

I have no idea why schools continue to push kids to the next grade knowing they are not prepared. I'm beginning to think they are purposely setting their kids up to fail so that they can apply for grants and federal aid based on their students' poor performance. It may become a great idea for federal agencies to require growth to receive additional funding.

I was on a mission to prove a point; therefore, I was hell-bent that my students were going to make significant gains for the year. To tackle our fluency problem, I applied for a grant to get them Reflex Math, which they loved. Reflex Math is technology that is quite innovative. It provides short practice sessions for students to improve their fluency, and my students needed a lot of work to increase theirs. Fluency greatly impacts a student's performance. Research has shown that when students can retrieve their basic facts fluently, they have more success in mathematics, especially on assessment items (tests).

Reflex Math was phenomenal!

I initially had some resistance; however, it was rapidly overcome. They realized fairly quickly that the option to not complete my assignments did not exist. Either they completed them during the allocated time, or they completed them during recess or activity. Either way, my work would get done every day! To hold the students accountable for completing the program daily, they were given a weekly grade for Reflex Math. They earned 20 points a day for a total of 100 points for the week. In no time, students were showing daily improvements in their basic math skills (addition, subtraction, multiplication, and division). Every time my students hit a milestone in the program, they were given a certificate, which I posted on the ceiling for everyone to see.

My students were not particularly fond of our reading program, and neither was I. It was too advanced. This was the problem that most of our kids faced. They were given materials on their grade level, which was a major problem since the majority of our students were not on grade level. I knew I had to increase my students' Lexile Levels, but my paying a little over $6K for the program would have resulted in me getting a divorce. My hubby would have killed me. If I had not already sneaked and spent a little over $2K for my classroom tables, I probably could have gotten away with it.

I did a little research and came across Reading A-Z. I liked the fact that the program was leveled, and it also had running records that could be completed online. I was hooked. To motivate the kids to complete their levels, they again received a grade. I also decided to make a bulletin board to track the progress. I placed yellow round plates on my bulletin board with the levels and then made a rocket for each student. Every time their levels increased, their rocket moved to the next level. Each time they leveled up, I added a star to their rocket. My two babies in the fourth grade who came to me on a

BR (Beginning Reader) reading level, rapidly moved up.

Like their teacher, my babies loved competition. I challenged them in my classroom by creating multiple opportunities for them to compete. Not only did they earn $20 scholarships for all A's, but they also earned numerous prizes and incentives to boost their academics.

During my first year, I mentioned to George the possibility of us having academic competitions, such as "the homeroom (or individual) with the highest accelerated reader points" or "individuals with the highest SRI scores." I even begged to be able to create Lexile clubs that students could become a member of once they met their milestone targeted Lexile Levels. I promised I would create and supply the school with dog tags for those students who met these achievements, but all of my suggestions were shut down or ignored. Even my offer to sponsor a limo to take eight of our students (those with the highest SRI growth and highest Lexile Levels) to Applebee's for lunch every nine weeks was nixed. I knew that would motivate our kids to read. What individual wouldn't be motivated by a limo ride?

I don't think anyone seriously expected the massive gains my class made for the year. Those two fourth graders who came to me on a BR Lexile Level increased by over 400 Lexiles. Two of my fifth graders increased 500 Lexiles. Everybody in that classroom increased significantly in reading. If they had only taken the Georgia Milestone seriously, our year would have been perfect.

ITS ALL ABOUT EXPECTATIONS

Many research studies have shown that low teacher expectations for minority students lead to greater difficulty for minority students to succeed in school. Google "expectations for black students" and multiple articles on this subject will appear. One article that caught my eye discussed a Johns Hopkins study that found when evaluating black students, white teachers expect less from them academically than their black counterparts.

Researchers analyzed data from an ongoing Educational Longitudinal Study that is following 8,400 tenth grade public school students. In the survey, two teachers (one white and one black) were asked to predict how far one particular student would go in school. The study, co-authored by Seth Gershenson and Stephen B. Holt from American University, found that both teachers pretty much rated the white students the same; however, when it came to their black students, the ratings differed greatly.

The white teachers had much lower expectations for black students, especially black boys. The black female teachers were significantly more optimistic about the ability of black boys to complete high school than teachers of any demographic group, including black male teachers. Ironically, black male teachers were found to have lower expectations for black male students than even white female teachers. I knew this was indeed a possibility because I had witnessed this happening in my own classroom with my assistant, Charles.

I truthfully believe that the expectations for minority students in the South, in general, are almost nonexistent, and it is seriously hurting their achievement. In many places I have taught in Georgia, it was evident that minority students were simply not expected to achieve. Over the past few years, I have witnessed this phenomenon more and more. This in itself is not harmful if the students are being reared in a household where they have role models who can neutralize their teacher's low expectations. In other words, if they have someone at home who can encourage them, then the possible discouragement that they receive from their teacher will not affect them as much.

This is why mentoring programs for the students who come from low socio-economic households without proper role models is so important. These kids must have someone who believes in them. In the absence of such figures in their lives, the low expectations for minority students often lead to self-fulfilling prophecies for these students.

A self-fulfilling prophecy occurs when a person unknowingly causes a prediction to come true because he/she expects or believes it to come true. In this instance, when teachers labeled their students inferior, lazy, dumb, bad, etc., and treated them as such, it fostered these behaviors in their students who had been subject to these expectations; thereby, it created a self-fulfilling prophecy.

The students in my class were more than capable of achieving academically and behaviorally. It all boiled down to expectations. I believed the reason my students had not been successful prior to entering my class was because their teachers and our administrators did not expect them to achieve or behave. To me, they were creating a self-fulfilling prophecy. They were unknowingly treating my students as if they were unable to achieve or behave, and their treatment fostered this behavior in my students.

I believed that these students could achieve exponentially, and that is how I treated them every day. Rather than telling them a daily laundry list of things they could not do or achieve, I constantly maintained high expectations for them and did not accept anything less. They didn't have any other choices but to succeed in my classroom.

Don't get me wrong; we had knockdown, drag-out fights some days, but I refused to amend my high expectations. There were many days I did not have a planning period because I was stuck in the room with a student, or students, who had not completed an assignment or had decided to misbehave during class. I couldn't place all of the blame on my fellow teachers. Even though they had allowed my students to refuse to learn and misbehave, my students knew their actions were wrong.

14 FROM EIGHTY-SIX TO ZERO

During one of our data meetings with the cohort who was monitoring my class, my principal mentioned in passing that 13 of my students had amassed a total of 86 out-of-school suspensions (OSS) for the prior year. Clearly, I had not heard him correctly, so I asked, "How many did you say?"

George replied, "Eighty-six."

Wow! So now he decided to finally fess up. I knew my students had been sent to the office multiple times the year before, but I didn't realize the magnitude. There had been 147 OSS incidents that year, and 86 belonged to my crew. My new mission was to ensure that the number of OSS referrals for my class remained zero. Here was another challenge I was looking forward to that year.

I was a strong disciplinarian, which was a major turnaround from my first year in education. I was probably one of the worst new teachers when it came to discipline. I knew the subject matter and could deliver lessons with ease, but discipline was another beast in itself for me. I wasn't prepared for the shift that had occurred in students' behavior. It had only been six years since I had graduated from high school and ten years since I had left elementary school. I don't know what had occurred during that decade, but I did know my classmates and I never misbehaved in such a manner in school.

My mother ultimately helped me become the disciplinarian that I am today. My mother, Mrs. Linda Gosier, taught school for 34 years. All of her former coworkers, parents, and students can attest to her being a top-notch teacher and strong disciplinarian at school and in our home. Momma worked with me on different disciplinarian strategies until I finally mastered the art of discipline. I knew, without a doubt, that I was finally a top-notch disciplinarian like my momma.

Most people tell new teachers not to smile until Christmas and be mean to the kids. Doing these things will make your life miserable rather quickly. I smiled a lot and often laughed with my students, which let them know I was human, too. First on my agenda almost every year was to assign my parents the first homework assignment. They had to tell me in a million words or less everything I needed to know about their child to ensure that our year was a great one.

I could tell a lot about my parents from that assignment. Some parents took their assignment seriously. They would type the assignment or legibly write pages about their child. I knew these were my parents who would be extremely supportive. Then I had parents who wrote only two or three sentences or a brief paragraph about their child. I knew these were my parents who were probably leading a busy life, and they would probably be semi-involved. Lastly, there were the parents who didn't bother to even complete the assignment, even after I called to remind them on several occasions. These were the students I knew I would probably have to become their momma for the year, which I honestly did not mind.

The major discipline problem plaguing my students was a lack of anger management. They would get upset and mad within sixty seconds, and it was amazing how small things would get them riled up. The funny thing was they would usually calm down within 15 minutes if no one escalated the situation, which is what their teachers in the past had done. Once they cooled down, it was as if nothing had ever happened. Most of them blew up as a tactic to avoid completing work they knew they would have difficulty completing. Once they realized all I wanted them to do was try whether they got the assignment correct or not, their whole demeanors began to change.

I strongly believe in consequences for behavior.

Without consequences, the behavior will not change. I allowed the students to come up with our classroom rules and the consequences that would incur if they chose not to follow them. Their consequences were so harsh I had to help them back off them a little. It always amazed me how every time I had done this activity over the years, my students were harder on themselves than I was.

After our rules and consequences were set in stone, I followed them religiously. I also incorporated many nonverbal cues, such as raising two fingers to signal I was done with a conversation. Once my two fingers were raised, the conversation was over, and I only wanted to hear, "Yes, ma'am," or "No, ma'am," after that point.

My favorite discipline tool was my discipline contracts. I would be so amused by the things the students would come up with in these contracts.

For instance, I had one student "agree to stop losing his temper when he could not get his way or when he was told no!" In our contract, I agreed to allow the student five minutes to compose himself by:

a) removing himself from the situation by going to the timeout corner outside of Dr. McCluskey's classroom;

b) laying his head down on the table for five minutes, and/or

c) walking four laps around the hallway, without tearing anything off the walls.

It seemed as if the students were more apt to follow the rules and accept the consequences without hesitation when they had input in the process.

Students are extremely astute. They figure out quickly what they can and cannot get away with and who they can and cannot manipulate with their bad behaviors. Even my son, Derrick, had figured out he could get over on his teacher while in kindergarten. Building a meaningful relationship with their parents becomes beneficial in the long run as well. Most of our students did not behave in the presence of their parents the way they behaved at school. Once I realized this, I shared this information with my principal. I said that our parents had far more control over their kids than the teachers assumed.

Several months later, after George bumped into the family of one of our students who was a hot mess, he told me, "Dr. McCluskey, you were right. They acted nothing like they act here!"

I replied, "That is why I go out of my way to build a rapport with my parents."

George didn't know it, but my students thought I had the power to suspend students. I overheard a student on the bus telling another student, "You better stop playing. Dr. McCluskey can suspend students!" The students probably believed this because I had sent for my parents to pick up their child when needed. I only had to do this a couple of times at the beginning of the year until my students caught on to the fact that I was serious about them behaving in my classroom.

I loved my parents! Every month, I hosted a parents'

dinner for them. At these meetings, I would share things we were working on in class, and we would informally chat about their kids and the community in general. I believed that these meetings kept a lot of my students' behaviors at bay. I would often remind my students that I didn't mind "snitching" on them when it was time for one of our dinners. Furthermore, they knew my "pull up game" was also quite strong. In other words, I would visit their houses as needed at the drop of a dime.

Our class ended the school year with me writing zero student referrals. Our school ended the year with only 58 OSS referrals. This was a decrease of 89 OSS for the year. This was an amazing difference. Our student discipline score for CCRPI increased from 79.735 to 92.766, and our school increased from a three-star climate rating to four stars. George acknowledged to me that the DLL had greatly impacted the discipline in our school. I am sure my haters will claim otherwise. They will probably say that the dramatic changes were a result of our Positive Behavior Intervention System (PBIS), the same program that was implemented the year before when AKD accumulated 147 OSS!

15 KNOW YOUR RIGHTS

A couple of months before my second year at AKD was coming to an end, one of my parents called me and asked for my assistance with her son, Charlie. Sharon informed me that she was at her wit's end and needed help. We had a close relationship because I had taught her oldest daughter, Carla, the year before and was teaching her other daughter, Karen, that year. I was only three years older than Sharon's mom who had passed away earlier the previous year, so I was like a mother figure to her and often provided her guidance. Like me, she didn't have any major problems with her daughters, just her son who was then in the first grade. That year, it seemed as if she had been called to come up to the school almost every day.

Parents of students in my Digital Learning Lab

(DLL) were ecstatic that they no longer had to be worried about the daily phone calls and multiple suspensions. I handled all of the discipline problems in our classroom. Unfortunately, there were far too many teachers in our building who relied on the office to handle their classroom discipline problems rather than handle the issues themselves. I could no longer feel sorry for those teachers because my year with the DLL students had proven that our difficult kids did indeed know how to behave. They were being allowed to behave otherwise. It irritated me how some of the teachers allowed our students to misbehave without correcting their behaviors. It was as if they believed our students were supposed to behave in a manner inappropriate for school simply because they were from low socio-economic homes. It was sad.

Sharon was frustrated because the school was calling her so much that she feared she was about to lose her job again. She had already lost one job several months earlier because the school called her repeatedly at work. Her employers had worked with her initially. However, as the calls increased in frequency, they decided to let her go. What irritated me most was the fact that Charlie had not displayed any of these behaviors when he was in kindergarten, nor did he display these behaviors when he was with me. This was clear evidence that the child may not entirely have been the problem.

In kindergarten, Charlie had been in Ms. Roper's class, and the parent may have received two phone calls the entire year. Ms. Roper was a hell of a kindergarten teacher with impeccable discipline. Parents wanted their kids in her class because they knew their children were going to be academically engaged and also learn how to behave properly. It was no secret that Ms. Roper was strict. She and I were quite similar in that regard.

This particular school year, his first-grade teacher was a veteran teacher who had been at the school for some time. She was one of those teachers who would frequently contact the office to handle discipline problems for her. I didn't particularly care for how she treated her students. It was as if she would pick and chose who she liked, and if she didn't like a student, it seemed as if they had a target on their back. In other words, to me, she made their lives miserable, which is a horrible experience for a first grader. It has been proven time and time again that childhood trauma causes multiple problems later in life for those who experience it, and this trauma can and frequently occurs in a school setting.

After I spoke with Sharon, I went to George and Louise and asked that they please contact me if they had any problems with this parent's son. I explained that Sharon was living with a friend because she was technically homeless. I was helping her find a place of her own, so it was important that she worked. It was extremely important that she did not lose another job because of their constant phone calls. George assured me that they would do their best to work with her and me.

A week or so later, I bumped into Sharon while

taking some of my students home who had remained after school for our Diamonds and Pearls meeting. Diamond and Pearls was the group I created for my girls. They met bi-monthly to learn life skills. I hadn't heard from Sharon since our earlier conversation, so I asked, "How's the job going?"

Sharon responded, "I lost it."

"Why?" I knew the administrators had not said anything to me about her son's behavior, so I assumed he had been behaving and was not the cause of her job loss.

Sharon informed me that Louise told her that she could not bring her son to school until after 10:00 a.m. each day. Because of this new requirement, she had to quit her job.

I was livid.

"Did you guys meet?" I asked.

"No. She just told me bring him later because they didn't want him to come to school until his medicine kicked in."

I was so sick and tired of school systems taking advantage of black parents who were not aware of their rights. Charlie had an Individualized Education Program (IEP) which meant there was supposed to have been a meeting in regards to any placement changes. No meeting had occurred; thus, the school was violating her son's rights as it pertained to the Individuals with Disabilities Education Act (IDEA). If the school wanted to make any changes to this child's services or placement, they were supposed to have informed this parent in writing. She also had "stay put" rights, meaning she could have requested he stayed put until they figured things out, which would have allowed her to keep her job.

There is nothing appropriate about telling a parent that they cannot bring their son to school until 10:00 a.m. because you don't want him in your school building until his medicine kicks in. This was ludicrous, especially since her son could have sat in my room and done his schoolwork until *his medicine kicked in.* I never had problems with this child whether he was medicated or not. I stated point blank that her rights were being violated, and I was going to call the special education director right then and there to make him aware of this situation. Louise supposedly had a special education background, so there was no way in the world she couldn't have realized she was blatantly breaking a federal law!

IDEA is a federal law that was first passed in 1975. Its primary purpose is to give children with disabilities from birth to age 21, the right to a free and appropriate education. IDEA requires schools to find and evaluate students suspected of having a disability, at no cost to their parents. Parents can also request to have their child evaluated if they suspect the child may have a disability. Once students are identified as having a disability, then the school has to provide them with special education and related services (speech therapy, counseling, etc.) to meet their needs. The goal of IDEA is to assist these students in making progress in school.

It is important to note that NOT all children with learning and attention issues are eligible for special education. Students must be disabled in one of 13 disability categories to qualify: autism, deaf-blindness, deafness, emotional disturbance, hearing impairment, intellectual disability, multiple disabilities, orthopedic impairment, other health impairment (including ADHD), specific learning disability (including dyslexia, dyscalculia, and dysgraphia, and other learning issues), speech or language impairment, traumatic brain injury, and visual impairment, including blindness. Just having one of these disabilities will NOT automatically qualify a child for special education services under IDEA. To be eligible for special education services, a student must have a disability, and as a result of that disability need special education to make progress in school. This means if the child has a disability, but is doing well in school, he/she may not be covered by IDEA and not be eligible for special education services.

If a child is determined to be eligible for special education services, then he/she is given, by law, an **Individualized Education Program (IEP).** An IEP is a LEGAL document for students age three through high school graduation or a maximum age of 22 (whichever comes first). The IEP addresses each child's individual learning issue and includes their specific educational goal. This document is legally binding, which means the

school must abide by the accommodations it promises in the document. By law, every IEP must include the following:
- The child's present level of performance (a description of the child's current abilities, skills, weaknesses, and strengths);
- Results of the child's evaluations and tests (including district-wide and state assessments);
- Supplementary aids and services (might include one-on-one aide, highlighted classroom notes, or assistive technology);
- The child's annual educational goals;
- Special education services that the school will provide the child to meet their annual educational goals;
- Modification/accommodations that the school will provide to help the child make progress in school;
- Accommodations that the child will be allowed when he/she takes their standardized tests, such as the Georgia Milestone;
- How and when the school will measure the child's progress as it pertains to their annual goals; and
- Depending on the child's age, transition planning that prepares teens for life after high school.

If a child is denied services under IDEA, all is not

lost; he/she may qualify for services under a different law called **Section 504 of the Rehabilitation Act**, a civil rights law. Although the **504 plan** is not a legally binding document or part of special education, it is a formal plan for students with learning and attention issues who do not need special education or individualized instruction, but they still need support and services to help them succeed in school. A student is eligible for Section 504 if the child has a physical or mental condition that substantially limits "a major life activity."

Major life activities for school children include learning, talking, breathing, caring for oneself, etc. In 2008, the reauthorization of the Americans Disabilities Act included additional conditions such as reading, concentrating, thinking, communicating with others, and major bodily functions. As of 2009, students taking medication to manage their ADHD can no longer be disqualified from having a 504 plan.

Many students have been diagnosed with ADD (Attention Deficit Disorder) or ADHD (Attention Deficit Hyperactivity Disorder). A 504 plan could greatly benefit these children. Appropriate accommodations that may be included in a Section 504 Plan include, but are not limited to:
- Reducing the number of homework problems (without reducing the level or content of what is being taught);
- Giving students a copy of notes;
- Creating a communication notebook so that

parents and teachers may keep each other informed of the child's progress or difficulties;
- Providing extra time on tests, etc.

Ironically, when I was the graduation coach at Thomasville High School, there were almost sixty kids with 504 Plans at the Scholar's Academy. Their parents had requested them for their children to enable them to receive extra testing time on their standardized tests (End of Course Tests (EOCT), SAT, ACT, etc.). At AKD, with all of the ADHD/ADD and ODD (Oppositional Defiance Disorder) diagnoses we had floating throughout our building, not one child had a 504 plan—nada, none, zilch, zero!

As promised, when I returned to the school, I called the central office and asked to speak to our director of special education, Mr. Trevor Metzger. I informed Mr. Metzger of the situation, and he asked me if he could meet with me that afternoon. I typically stayed late after school, so I stated that it was no problem to meet him at school.

He did.

Mr. Metzger asked me to contact Sharon during our meeting. I was able to reach her and allowed him to speak with her via speakerphone. She shared with him the same information she had with me, and it was evident he was somewhat shocked. He had no clue of the violations against this parent and her son were taking place, and it soon came to light that this parent was not the only parent who had been experiencing these illegal changes in placement. There were others who were being told to not come to school until their medicine kicked in, or they could only come to school for a half day and had to be picked up early.

Mr. Metzger assured Sharon that what occurred with her was not standard policy, and he apologized for what she had endured. He informed her that he would personally be scheduling a meeting as soon as possible and would have held the meeting the next day, but he already had another engagement, and so did the parent. It was decided that the meeting would be held the upcoming Friday. Before she got off the phone, Sharon requested I also be allowed to attend the meeting, which Mr. Metzger assured her would be no problem.

Parents need to understand that they have the right to bring someone knowledgeable with them to an IEP meeting or any meeting that concerns their child. If a parent doesn't fully understand what's going on at their child's school, they do not have to go to the school alone. They need to find someone trustworthy and knowledgeable to assist in any meetings. My aunt, Mrs. Hattie Bull, taught in Delaware for years as a high school English teacher. She shared with me that many of their parents also claimed intimidation was the reason that they did not come out to their child's school. To assist these parents, ministers in the community formed a group to act as advocates for their parents. These ministers would accompany parents who asked for assistance with their son or daughter's school meetings.

That Friday, we all met in George's office, and true to his word, Mr. Metzger had a solution that would satisfy the parent and provide assistance with the student.

16 UP, UP, AND AWAY!

I couldn't wait until the last day of school, and it wasn't because of the situation with my assistant principal. I felt Louise was upset with me because I had reported Charlie's violations to Mr. Metzger. I had prayed about that situation; when I prayed about something, I turned it completely over to God. I had learned to allow Him to handle situations. I was excited because I was about to fly 43 of my students and parents to Washington, D.C.

That February, I had been teaching a geography lesson and became hysterical when the students couldn't tell me the names of states that I know they should have known. I shared with them the names of states I had lived in or visited. As I pointed them out, I stopped on Maryland. I told them all about the state and mentioned how I used to fly back and forth from Maryland to

Georgia all of the time. As I was telling them about the time my kids took pictures in the cockpit with the pilot, I realized from the expressions on their faces that they didn't have a clue as to what I was talking about. I asked who had flown before and no one had.

I was determined to change that! On my birthday, I posted a message on my Facebook page. I asked all of my friends to give me $4.50 or $45.00 for my birthday to help fly us to D.C. I have some of the best friends ever! Many of them offered to pay for a student's entire plane ticket, which was around $180. With the money I raised, I was able to pay for 14 students' tickets. No one in my class had to pay to fly to Washington, D.C.

My assistant, Charles, suggested that we also take our Distinguished Gentlemen group as well, and I thought that would be a fantastic idea. However, it was agreed that the gentlemen who were not in my class and their parents would pay for their own tickets, which they didn't mind doing. Everyone was thrilled to be able to fly to Washington, D.C.

Initially, the plan was for our group to fly to D.C., eat lunch at the airport, and then fly back to Atlanta-Hartsfield. This initial plan morphed into something on a larger scale. After Charles spoke with a friend of his named Dr. Herschel Holiday who lived in D.C., it was decided that we would also tour D.C. via a chartered bus. His friend, Dr. Holiday, who was a retired United States Army General, was sponsoring our bus. Dr. Holiday was a product of the Rome City School System and a West

Point graduate. He had led a successful career. I told my students that Dr. Holiday was living proof that they, too, could become a success story one day. His skin was the color of theirs, and he had also come from humble beginnings like them. But, he didn't allow any of those circumstances to stop him from reaching his goals.

The most exhilarating of the entire trip was our takeoff. As the plane taxied down the runway and began to lift into the air, our students raised their hands above their heads. They didn't make any noise, so I didn't realize what they were doing until my daughter, who was sitting next to me, asked, "Momma, why are they putting their hands in the air?"

I was so tickled. I guess going up in an airplane does feel as if you are riding on a roller coaster. I turned to the passengers sitting around us and said, "It's our first time flying!" They awed us, and it was smooth sailing from there.

I was so proud of my babies! We had undeniably come a mighty long way in a year's time.

Touring D.C. with these students made me realize exactly how much social studies I did not learn in school. Our tour guide was fantabulous and should have been a history teacher. He was a treasure trove of knowledge.

Though we didn't get an opportunity to tour it, we saw the new African American Museum. From there, we rode by the Washington Monument and made a stop at the Lincoln Memorial. The kids were so excited when they realized that they were standing in the same spot as

Dr. Martin Luther King had when he gave his famous "I Have a Dream" speech.

It gave me goose bumps.

From the Lincoln Memorial, we jetted to the Capitol. We saw the theater where President Lincoln was shot, and the house next door where he died. We visited so many other significant places around D.C. that I lost track of them. The one place I knew the students would never forget visiting was the White House. The students were given an opportunity to walk down the street to the White House and take pictures.

Our trip to Washington, D.C. was one that the students and their parents will never forget. I know I won't.

On our way back from Washington, D.C., Charles encouraged me to apply for the principal's job since we had recently learned that George would be promoted to middle school principal position. I stated what a waste of time that would be but promised him I would apply just for the heck of it. Over the past two years, I had applied for the assistant principal positions at the middle and high school, interviewed for both, and had not been offered either. If I couldn't get an assistant principal's position, why on God's green earth would I even fathom getting a job as a principal?

I told him, "This upcoming school year, I plan to accomplish more than my previous two years in the system."

One thing about me, I don't get bitter because of

disappointments in my life; I get better. It took me years to get to the point where I realized that when disappointments occur, they are God's way of getting my attention. Once He has my attention, He sends the blessings my way; I cannot rush His greatness.

I didn't realize just how upset Louise was with me, until Charles asked me to check her Facebook page to read a post she had written about our trip. Apparently, Louise was tracking our flight and had posted a Facebook message that she was glad about our safe return. As I tried to see the post that Charles wanted me to see, I realized that Louise had unfriended me after I reported her to Mr. Metzger about Charlie's rights being violated.

Wow!

Imagine my dismay when a few weeks later, the word on the street was our new superintendent, Patrick, had promised her George's job. I knew if she was petty enough to unfriend me on social media, I was now in some serious hot water and undeniably in Louise's crosshairs. At that point, I decided if she was made the principal of our school, I was resigning. There was no way I was going to work for her. I had dealt with the likes of her in Cedartown, and I refused to deal with anything similar ever again.

17 TIME FOR A CHANGE

On the morning of June 1, 2017, I woke up determined to make trouble. I was tired of business as usual and didn't particularly care whose toes I stepped on that day. I had reentered the field of education four years ago, and I still couldn't believe how blatantly segregated we still were; children of color were being miseducated, and politics had evaded education at all levels. Public education was broken, and I was ready to walk away! After almost nineteen years in this field, it seemed as if things were becoming worse rather than better.

My frustration was further compounded by the rumor mill, which was in overdrive. According to the street committee, Louise was indeed going to be our new principal. George had moved on up, and it seemed as if Louise was trying to move up with him. From the way Louise had been acting the last few weeks of school, it was fairly evident that she had the job. She had already informed me that next year I was to "stay in my lane," whatever that meant! Thanks to me having jury duty the last week of school, I escaped the planning meetings that everyone else on our staff had been forced to attend. From the documentation I read after I returned for post planning, it was *expected that teachers work within their duties and responsibilities as classroom teachers.* The key term being *within.* Now I understood what she meant by *I needed to stay in my lane.* She hated when teachers sent their students to my room to be disciplined. Assisting my peers with discipline was viewed as being in the administrator's (her) lane.

George and Louise failed to realize that if they had disciplined the students for the teachers, I would not have had to step into their lanes and do their jobs. Our students were not afraid to take themselves to their offices at will, whereas they would attempt to hide in the restroom to keep from coming to my room. They knew they would not be given a coloring sheet and an iPad when they came to see me. Those were the toys they received when they took themselves to the office, which was different from what they received when their teachers sent them to my room. I gave them a behavior letter to write, and my behavior letters were unforgettable as evidenced by a student I taught ten years ago. She posted her behavior letter from back then onto Facebook and tagged me. I couldn't believe she had kept my letter all of those years.

Over the past school year, I had proven that not only

could black children learn exponentially, they could also behave when provided guidance and structure. All these children needed were more caring teachers who saw them as being more than a stereotype. They needed to see more people who looked like them in positions higher than mine. I decided it was time to rattle a few cages to see what happened, and what better way to do that than a Facebook post.

> *I submitted a FOIA request to see exactly who applied for our principal's position at my school, Anna K. Davie Elementary! I am so close to finally walking away from education because I am soooo tired of business as usual! I didn't play games when I was a child, so I definitely do not see myself playing them now! We must select the best individuals for administration positions, not friends or those who are good politicians! Ultimately, it is the leader who plays a pivotal role in a school's success! I'm tired of having the lowest scores in the system when our problems can be easily solved! I'm tired of children of color being shortchanged!!! We need at least one of our leaders to be Black! I'm not going to try to sugar coat it any longer, our students need DIVERSITY, especially at the top!! When I took my job two years ago, there was only one black teacher in a building that is comprised of 98 percent Black and Hispanic students, mainly black! This year, four more black teachers were hired on a certified staff of almost 50 but still no black academic coaches, counselors, assistant principal, or principal! How can this system even justify having seven elementary schools (now six)*

with all white principals, all white assistant principals in all but one, all white academic coaches, and all white counselors in a system that is only 35 percent white? If my school was all white and the teacher population, assistant principal, counselor, and principal were all black, eyebrows would be raised! Yet, when we have buildings full of black kids and no teachers who look like them, it's okay! We need diversity!!! These kids need people who can culturally understand them! I proved that vividly this year with my class. Stop claiming that black teachers and administrators cannot be found! If I have to make a FOIA request for every position posted, I will to prove a point that there are quality black applicants, and Rome City can hire black teachers and administrators if they truly wanted to make things more diverse!! Diversity benefits us all. We can learn from each other!!! Since it appears nothing is addressed until you bring it to the surface, I'm going on the record: One of our administrative positions need to be filled with a person of color! It will never have to be me; I am content to collect my $76K to teach 16 students or 40. What message do we send to our students of color when they never see people of color in higher positions?

These are solely my opinions and do not reflect my employment! If they did, I would not have to post this message. Candidates will be shared as soon as I retrieve this package. And yes, I AM

TIRED of bull crap!!!

#allkidsmatter!!!!

Several coworkers reached out to me and commended my bravery in speaking out. I warned them to not respond to my posts. My speaking out about different ills had made me a target on more than one occasion, and I didn't want that to happen to any of them. In the Facebook group that I had created just for our faculty and staff, All We Have is Each Other, I posted a message for my colleagues:

Guys,

Please do not feel obligated to like or respond to my posts about the system. I know it's easy for teachers to be retaliated against, and you can't afford that when you are the only breadwinner or can't live without your income. I used to be that teacher! I never spoke up, because I knew that I needed my job!!! I sat back and watched things that I knew were wrong, but I had no choice but to remain quiet. I enjoy nice things... 😊

Now that my business brings in more than my salary, I can finally use my voice to speak up and fight for what's right!!! I'm not, by any means, trying to discredit any of you. I often share with my former teachers back home about how much our teachers genuinely care about our students; however, the fact that these kids need more diversity cannot be ignored. Here I am an educated individual who had no idea what a koozie was. Why? My culture doesn't typically use that word.

It's the same with our kids. The great thing is, if willing, we can all learn from each other.

I'm frustrated because I know our school can be better! Many of our kids are getting over because of cultural" differences. If nothing else, my class proved that this year. They know how to behave; they simply choose not to because they are exploiting the cultural loophole. They are too young to understand the value of education; thus, my desire to raise expectations! It pains me knowing that an education could lift these kids out of poverty; yet, the students are being allowed to make choices that most can't make at their house! I think you guys know me well enough by now to know that I keep it 💯; however, my intent is never to offend or make anyone feel bad. If I have done either with my posts, please accept my sincerest apologies because all we have is each other! ♥

I knew some people were probably offended by my Facebook post. But I didn't care then, and I still could care less now. My post spoke the truth, and if the roles were reversed, whites would be outraged. Imagine a school of all white students being taught by almost all black teachers. That scenario has not occurred and probably will never occur in the United States; yet, the majority sees absolutely nothing wrong with having primarily black schools staffed with primarily white teachers. It's wrong in that it hurts minority students. There were so many behaviors that minority students engaged in during my prior two years at AKD that my white counterparts did not see as wrong because, in their minds, it was the *expected* behavior of black kids. Being black and understanding the black culture, I knew that our kids knew better and held them to a higher standard. I couldn't even say the expectations for minorities were low; for many teachers, they were simply nonexistent.

Diversity is important in our schools. When schools are staffed with diverse teachers, they are able to pull from each other's collective experiences and cultural norms. This is how the negative stereotypes become dispelled. There are always opportunities to learn from each other. For instance, while talking to Ms. Roper's student teacher one day, I heard a term that was not familiar to me. Ms. Couch told the two of us that she would make us a koozie with our sorority names on it.

We both looked at her and asked, "What is a koozie?"

Ms. Couch laughed and asked us, "You guys honestly don't know what a koozie is?"

We replied in unison, "No!"

She pulled up a picture of a koozie on Ms. Roper's smartboard. At that point, Ms. Roper and I laughed. I explained to Ms. Couch that we, meaning most blacks, didn't call that item a koozie. In our circles, what she had shown us was a can or beer holder. All of us learned something new from each other that day.

After my post, I was deemed "pro-black." I was not shocked in the least. I had been deemed pro-black ten years earlier when I taught in Cedartown, so to be labeled that again was no surprise. The sad thing was those who genuinely knew me were well aware of the fact that I advocated for all children regardless of their skin tone. I had come to realize that anytime I acted in the best interest of black children, I would be labeled pro-black, which was unintelligent. I would be a hypocrite if I didn't advocate for the children of color. If not me, then who?

My assistant, Charles, had already informed me that I was unique in that I actually cared about our AKD kids. According to him, most influential blacks who were able to reach back and help our kids wouldn't, and there appeared to be much truth to his statement.

When I first pondered the idea of starting a charter school, I approached two prominent black preachers in Rome and asked them would they be willing to be on the founding board. They both informed me that they needed to "pray about it." One of the ministers was frequently in our school and should have been well aware of the disparities our kids faced since many attended this pastor's church. They each had to pray about forming a charter school to help our youth receive a quality education; yet, I looked in the newspaper and there they were at public functions claiming to want to help our youth. I often wondered, did they honestly want to help, or were they more interested in public recognition?

My cousin, James C. Marable, is one of the most spiritual pastors I know. He is a Morehouse College graduate; his grasp of the ministry is above par. I was so bothered by these preachers' responses that I reached out to my cousin via Facebook messenger:

James C. Marable is, "Let me pray about it," the new method of preachers saying no? Give me the biblical background for this one. I'm dead serious.

He responded:

Hey, cuz, let me try to respond without painting with too broad of a paintbrush! I think you have to make a specific judgment based on the person you're dealing with! Not everyone operates by the same ethical code, and I know you know that very well! There are some pastors and people, in general, who use the proverbial, "Let me pray about it," in a disingenuous fashion, knowing very well they have no plans to get back with you! Personally, I believe in being honest with people up front. If I like your idea and think it's something I could participate in, I'll tell you. If I don't, I'll tell you that, too! Now, what I'm about to say next may sound unspiritual to some! I don't pray about everything, every time! I always pray and ask God for wisdom and discernment in every situation! This has allowed me to reach a place of maturity in my decision making! Life's experiences and wisdom received from others has matured my decision-making as well! So, when certain situations come up, I already have wisdom at work in my soul and can make an on the spot decision! There is nothing to pray about. Now, I may have to think about, yes—and I can give you a simple yes, no, or not at this time! Lastly, why do I need to seek God when He's given me common sense? I think you get my point! Whenever I sense someone trying to escape giving me an answer by saying, "Let me pray about it," I usually respond by saying, "What specifically do you have to pray about?" So, use your wisdom, cuz, and allow the spirit to enlighten you. You will know when the person is being genuine or fake! If you're sensing an individual being fake, just move on! If you feel they really are intent on seeking God, ask them, "When can I get back to you?   " Because the truth of the matter is if a person is that spiritual, it won't take them long to hear the voice of God! Hope this helps, cuz!

I moved on.

18 THE NEW PRINCIPAL

The teachers, parents, and students of AKD still had no idea who their new principal would be when June came. Speculation had been in the air for weeks that the assistant principal would be our new principal. We could also tell by Louise's demeanor that the job was possibly hers. I was waiting until the Rome City Board of Education met later in the month to determine if she was definitely going to have the job. I planned to resign the day after the meeting if the job was given to Louise.

The Saturday before the meeting was to be held, I received a call from a coworker informing me she had been told things were not going as we all had suspected. Apparently, the new administration had decided to go in another direction, and our new principal would now be a black guy from Atlanta.

I did not see that coming. None of us did.

It wasn't until Monday that I became aware of the fact I, or rather my Facebook post, was being blamed for Louise not getting the job. The truth of the matter is that it was not me, but her credentials should have been cited as the reason she didn't get the job. The new principal, who we now knew was Dr. Clifton Nicholson, came with impeccable credentials. Dr. Nicholson was a seasoned educator with over 17 years of experience. He was an assistant principal for the Atlanta Public School System, and this would be his first principal job.

My coworker called me again to tell me the rumor that our superintendent, Patrick, had promised her the job for the past six weeks was really true. Apparently, Louise allegedly told several people she had been given the job and then summoned to the board office that Thursday or Friday prior to the Tuesday board meeting and told it was no longer hers.

I was ecstatic Louise had not been given the job. Morale and discipline had been horrible for the past two years, and I didn't foresee things getting any better. Furthermore, the kids would now have a principal who looked like them. My only concern was that the Board was not moving Louise to another location, which I knew from past experiences was a recipe for disaster. I was terrified she would be on a mission to retaliate against me for my perceived role in the principal's selection.

I googled my new principal's name to see if I could find more information about him. He didn't have a social media presence, which was a good sign. After being unfriended on Facebook by Louise, I was beginning to believe administrators interacting with their subordinates on social media may not be such a good idea. As I scrolled through the pictures of the school where Dr. Nicholson was last an assistant principal, I caught sight of a familiar face, Lynn Jenkins.

Lynn Jenkins was a good friend of mine. She and I attended Fort Valley State College, where she was voted our Student Government Association's (SGA) president. We had known each other since 1990, so I trusted her judgment completely. When she validated that our board had made an excellent selection, I tore up my resignation letter. Finally, I felt that AKD could begin accomplishing more. On another note, I guess when this is published, Dr. Nicholson will finally learn that I did an "unofficial" background check on him.

I knew Dr. Nicholson was going to have his work cut out for him. Though the parents and students were ecstatic that he was coming, I figured our staff might be another problem. Since the board had left Louise assigned to our building, there were sure to be a few teachers who felt they would not seem loyal to her if they made the principal feel welcomed. Many of us couldn't believe or understand why the board didn't reassign her to the middle school with George, especially since Patrick had reneged on the job offer. I actually couldn't blame Louise for being riled; the central office had screwed this situation up royally.

Sometime around the end of June, I went to the school to retrieve some items from my classroom and bumped into Dr. Nicholson. Ms. Acquilla Askew, my coworker and good friend, was with me at the time. The two of us gave him a tour of our school and an impromptu tour of Rome's different sides.

Of course, we bumped into several students along the way, and most of them asked, "Who is that man in your car?"

I replied, "You know my baby brother that I talk about all the time? That's him."

Ms. Askew and I were tickled pink that they never did figure out that they had just met their new principal.

The first hint of trouble came via an email from Louise to me. I had sent her an email informing her that the AKD teachers had organized a surprise *meet and greet* for Dr. Nicholson during the second week in July. We needed her help to ensure he was in the building at that time. We also wanted her to present him with a gift basket and say a few words of welcome. The gesture was made in good faith because we did not want her to feel alienated in any way.

Louise responded:

> *Thanks for letting me know. I've been hearing about this for a couple of weeks. It is unfortunate that this is a time when the entire faculty and staff can't be present, but I'm sure it will be great for those who are here. I will do my best to ensure he is in the building. If you are inviting Patrick and*

Olive, and I'm sure they will avoid scheduling any meetings for him on his first day.

I'm so glad you got to meet him, introduce him to those who were here, and show him around the school and community. I look forward to meeting him. I know he is going to do a phenomenal job.

I informed my coworkers via our Facebook group:

Her response was not necessarily a yes, but what disturbs me is the, "I have been hearing about this for weeks!" I'm going on the record now to let everyone know that we are not going to be divided this year. We are not creating Team #louise or Team #drnicholson! I'm tired of the Democrats and Republicans mess!!! I will not work in an environment similar to our political climate. I'm a professional who knows how to separate my personal and professional feelings. Why wouldn't I include Louise? It takes the entire team to make our dream work!!! Our focus is and should always be these kids first, and everyone should want to increase our achievement and CCRPI scores!! I'm embarrassed that we are ALWAYS at the bottom. These kids can learn as proven by my students 400 and 500 increases in their Lexile scores!! So, to whoever ran to tell Louise about our meet and greet, please run or screenshot this! AKD is going to move up next year!! Dr. Nicholson didn't ask to become a part of any drama, so he will not be wasting his time mediating; He will be focusing on achievement!!! To everyone who has offered to participate and who are on board, your actions will let me see where your heart is! No weapons formed against our AKD Family will prosper! I promise you it won't work. All we have is each other!!!

A couple of days before the event, the faculty and staff received an email informing us that the building would be closed due to custodial work.

Really?

As I suspected, the year was going to be a long one.

I confirmed with the head custodian that we could still use the cafeteria for the event since we could enter this area through the office. After she confirmed, I asked the assistant principal to forward an email to the staff letting them know the surprise reception was still a go. Several staff members believed it had been canceled because of an email that had been sent about the building being closed. When Louise sent the email to the staff, she included Dr. Nicholson as well.

Oh, well, so much for our surprise reception!

19 THE FIRST MONTH

Before our first day of school, I posted a message to the faculty and staff via our Facebook group:

I am actually excited about this year and truly believe that God has blessed us with an AWESOME leader! Doc is humble, compassionate, willing to listen, and truly cares about what we have to say. Can you say, a breath of fresh air? There is a positive spirit permeating our building, and it gives me hope that we can finally make some much needed improvement! As we prepare for tomorrow, I want to wish everyone a blessed first day!! Let's shower each other with love this year. We may start this year at the bottom, but we definitely will not finish there!!! Remember, all we have is each other!!! #teamAKD!!

There was a consensus among many faculty and

staff members that the first week of school was one of the most peaceful starts we had ever experienced. There was a calmness throughout our building. Unfortunately, this turned out to be the calm before the storm. During the third week of school, I noticed some teachers had started sending an abnormal number of students out of their classes for minor infractions. I knew this because Charles had now become our new behavior specialist, and since he was stationed in my room, I could hear the chatter on the radio that he carried.

Suspiciously, when I had approached Mike, and George about the behavior specialist position the year prior, I was told they were not going to create the position. I would have thought my decreasing the referrals of the 13 students who had amassed 86 out-of-school suspensions in one year to zero would have proven I was the most qualified for the job. Charles did not accomplish that feat; I did. The only reason I allowed Charles to remain in my room was the fact that his aggravating the students gave me ample opportunities to teach them how to respond to adverse stimulus. I had even explained this to my students' parents on more than one occasion after receiving complaints from them about Charles.

Typically, I was the one who interacted with the students while he sat in one of my booths working on football stuff or talking on his phone. Being that Charles was close friends with Elaina and frequently corresponded with Faith and Will, two other board members, I was certain there was far more to this story. When I approached Dr. Nicholson about Charles being given the position, I found out that the decision had been made by others above his pay grade. I wasn't surprised in the least.

What hurt more was the fact that Charles had been well aware of the fact that I wanted to become our behavior specialist. Never-the-less, I chose to still work with him.

I posted a message to our faculty and staff in our group:

> *Charles is now the behavior specialist. All students should come to him before the office. He leaves at 1:00 p.m. every day. When he leaves, we should try to first seek help from a teammate before sending students to Dr. Nicholson. I'm trying to ascertain why so many students are being sent straight to Dr. Nicholson in the first place. I pray this is not purposeful. During my two years here, I don't recall students being sent to George in this manner. The principal is our last line of defense, not the first.*
>
> *Charles and I are creating a behavior plan for each student who has been deemed a problem student. He will meet with them starting Monday. Behavior will not deter our progress!!! #teamAKD*

If I felt frustrated, I was fairly certain Dr. Nicholson was feeling some type of way as well. I was trying to figure out what in the world was going on. Teachers who normally handled their own discipline were now acting like first-year teachers who needed assistance. To further compound matters, rumors were floating around that I was trying to become Dr. Nicholson's assistant principal next year. What in the world? We were only in the first month of school, and people were making plans for next year! It was disappointing to me.

Certain teachers were sending students to Dr. Nicholson's office persistently. Keep in mind I had the so-called behavior students in my classroom, so what was their excuse? And while all of this tomfoolery that started out of the blue was going on—where was our assistant principal, Louise? According to the kids, she was hiding out in the conference room of the library, which I later determined to have some merit.

Shame on the bright members of the Rome City Board of Education, Patrick, and his new assistant superintendent, Olive, who honestly believed that Louise would not have any hard feelings about the principal's job being yanked away from her. I felt horrible for Dr. Nicholson, the innocent victim, who was stuck in the middle of some bull crap he had not asked for. It seemed obvious that Louise was bitter, and I sincerely believed she was purposely dividing our staff into separate teams. I couldn't blame our teachers because she possessed positional power, which is why those who followed her were probably afraid of not doing so.

Louise's hiding out was despicable, but her ignoring the kids misbehaving in her presence was worse. One particular day, a student in my class came to me visibly distraught. Apparently, her little brother was running around the school like a wild person.

My student said she was upset because our assistant principal had not helped her stop her little brother. Even worse, the little brother had almost tumbled down the stairs.

"Are you serious?" I asked.

She replied, "Here is the video!" and proceeded to show me everything she had just described on video. Sure enough, the video showed the little boy running full speed past Louise, her not attempting to do anything and him almost tumbling down the stairs.

"Will you please go get him, Dr. McCluskey?" she pleaded.

I agreed, and when we stepped outside of my classroom, her little brother was running down our hall toward my classroom. I pointed to my door, and he ran into our class and sat down in one of my booths. I called his mom and asked her to come and get him.

Back to the group:

I have NO desire to be the assistant principal at Anna K. Davie next year or any other year! Life is too short for me to waste my time fighting with adults, who would rather attack me every chance they get than do what's best for our students. Hopefully, your knowing that I don't desire, want, or will not accept the job will ease some of your minds to the point that the attacks against me stop. I'm saved, but I'm also human and still a work in progress. I'm tired of the foolishness. [First-grade teacher] when you came to my room yesterday, I was truly having a horrible day. Ray Charles and Stevie Wonder both could have seen that. We scream PBIS [Positive Behavioral Interventions and Supports] for the students, let's scream that for the teachers as well! I don't enter anyone's room uninvited in our building. I would appreciate the same courtesy! Kay came after you sent her, and she was told to come back, too, which she politely agreed to do!

Yesterday, I had 14 behavior kids who were not mine in addition to the 18 who are mine. The Elm Street class like mine has ten kids and a paraprofessional!! In addition, I have not had a planning period in two weeks since I am watching kids as Charles goes to get more! I share this to give you a glimpse into my day! There are others who are experiencing far worse! So, before we continue running and telling on each other, talk to each other first! Furthermore, you guys didn't try all these shenanigans with me during George's watch!!

Just so we are clear, I do plan to become principal or CEO of Cornerstone Charter Academy when it opens in 19-20! This will be a drama free facility where kids will ALWAYS come first. Faculty will hire incoming faculty, and we will all work together as a family! Any problems will be resolved with ALL parties present in a timely manner!!

OAN: If you choose not to enter your Milestone Lexiles, I have no problems with that either. I'm still going to do for our kids regardless of the actions of the adults around them. You guys fail to understand that our TEM [Teacher Effectiveness Measure] scores are dependent upon our kids' performance. That score is given by the state and follows us wherever we go!! While digging that ditch for me, you may as well dig one for you, too!! I ain't going nowhere but up—when God elevates me in 19-20!!!

Feel free to screenshot and share! Everything else I post is shared that way!!

OVER BEFORE IT STARTS

Within the first month of school, Dr. Nicholson had approached me numerous times about complaints and concerns he had received. I was accused of failure to report an incident of suspected abuse that had occurred over the summer; the accused was in jail for what he had done. Clearly, this was not a reportable incident since it had already been taken care of by law enforcement. I was accused of making a coworker feel frightened; the same coworker who practically lived in my classroom near the end of last school year asking me for assistance with writing papers for her specialist degree. I was accused of so much until that particular day, he finally brought me a list of complaints so I could compose a response.

I had been at the school for two years and had no major complaints from parents, students, or coworkers. I prided myself on being able to get along with my coworkers and caring about their wellbeing. I was that person on our staff who went out of her way to ensure everyone was taken care of and enjoyed our work environment. I had spent hundreds of dollars buying resources to share with my coworkers. When I bought Vocabulary/Spelling City for my classroom, I bought it for the third grade teachers as well. I also sponsored our last Christmas party. After being told we were going to have a Christmas party for two years, and it never occurred, I was the one who sponsored a feast for the faculty and purchased stainless-steel bangles with charms representing each person's alma mater on them. During Teacher Appreciation Week, I spent hours creating handmade cards for each teacher to let them know they were appreciated. If teachers wanted to throw a popcorn party for their class for some achievement or another, I popped it and made sure it was delivered to them. I paid for my coworkers to accompany my class to Washington, D.C.

I was done!

I finally asked, "Exactly who is giving you all of these complaints and concerns?"

He informed me that all of the complaints against me had come from Louise, Kay and Betty, and no one else as I had suspected. I immediately felt better. I wasn't even upset with my coworkers because I realized that they were being used as pawns. I knew I would be retaliated against, but I didn't realize it was going to come so swiftly and with such vengeance.

I owed George a huge apology. I'm sure he had also

caught much hell because of me. There were plenty of times when these same three individuals had come after me, and George had made them back off. They had Dr. Nicholson between a rock and a hard place, and I am sure they knew it.

If he didn't continue to reprimand me almost daily, it would appear as if he was giving me preferential treatment, which they could say was due to my Facebook post supposedly getting him his job. I am sure they knew the constant complaints were going to eventually wear me down, and they did.

I thanked Dr. Nicholson for bringing me more concerns and promised to send him a response, which I did as follows:

The concern by teachers that I enter classrooms, other than my own, to discipline students.

First and foremost, I would still like to know which "teachers" had this concern, since there were several teachers ([1], [2], [3], [4], [5], [6], [7], [8], [9], [10], [11], [12] and so on) who reached out to me to handle "discipline" issues for them. Despite the fact that I promised you I would "stay in my lane," there are still several teachers who are reaching out to me to help them with discipline issues. Many of the teachers I work with have improved tremendously since the beginning of the year. The support group that Ms. Roper and I created appears to be helping them improve their classroom management. Several of the new teachers have thanked me for assisting them this year. In the final analysis, it truly takes a village to raise children. When I was growing up, everyone in my community disciplined my siblings and myself. The cafeteria worker, who was also my church's piano player, not only kept my mother informed about our behavior, she also disciplined us. I have no hesitations, reservations, and problems remaining in my lane, but will you please clarify whether or not I need to turn the teachers who seek help away? Since we are "documenting" concerns, I most definitely do not want to seem insubordinate in any manner.

The concern that my students do not follow the school's morning routines.

To address this concern, I spoke with [1], [2], [3], and Betty. It appears that Betty was the only person who had a concern with my students not following morning routines, which is a false accusation or simple lack of communication. I am fairly certain that Betty is well aware of the fact that I was asked by George to report to work earlier last year to keep my students from being in the hallway in the morning. He specifically informed me that he did not want my students in the hallway, if at all possible, due to their propensity to misbehave for other teachers. I was not informed this procedure had changed, and my students have been reporting straight to my classroom at 7:30 a.m. Upon arrival, the students complete their Reflex math (fluency) and SpellingCity (vocabulary) assignments on their Chromebooks silently. If you would like for my students to sit in the hallway until 7:45 each day, I will be more than happy to accommodate your request and leave novels outside for them to read.

I do not attend grade level meetings.

This is another false accusation. I have attempted to attend all grade level meetings this year. I missed Betty's grade level meeting due to having to attend an IEP meeting for Charlie. I emailed Betty asking for her to reschedule the meeting so that I could meet with her. She not only ignored my email, but she placed the information from the meeting in my box. Please see attached email.

I was late to Kay's grade level meeting because I had students who were not mine in my classroom. Charles had been called out of my room; therefore, I could not leave the kids unsupervised, which I informed Kay. To accommodate me, Kay came to my room and met with me there.

I record students with my cell phone.

I record my students with my cell phone and use the videos in my class to discuss inappropriate behavior. Students often do not realize how their actions look to others. When we watch video footage, we discuss in detail how they could have handled a situation more appropriately. This school has numerous cameras, but unfortunately, there are none in my classroom. Due to the nature of my classroom, it is important that I record my students' behavior. A prime example is a student that Charles and I dealt with the other day. He blatantly lied to his mother about our interaction. The mother was wholeheartedly believing him until I shared the video of his behavior with her. She then chastised her son about his behavior.

I am somewhat disheartened I had to even address concerns on August 10. The school year has just begun, and I sincerely feel these concerns were brought to you in an attempt to tarnish my reputation. I am sure these individuals did not share with you the numerous things I have done for this school, my parents, my colleagues, and my students.

In Matthew 6:4 (NIV), we are told to give, "so that [our] giving may be in secret," which is why I rarely publicize my "giving." However, since certain individuals have taken the opportunity to lambaste me to you, I would like to take this opportunity to also let you know what an asset I have been to our school. Below are some of the things I have done for AKD over the past two years:

- *Purchased all of the furniture (approximately, $2500) to turn my room into a cafe so that my students would not be ostracized for being placed in a behavior class;*
- *Purchased IXL ($349) and Kids A-Z ($199) for my students;*
- *Purchased Curriculum Associates testing resources ($400) for my students;*
- *Purchased numerous interactive notebook materials ($300) which I shared with all 3-6 grade teachers last year and many this year;*
- *Provided and will still provide $20 scholarships to every student in grades 3-6 who earn all A's each*

semester;

- *Sponsored our first ever "No C's" party for all students grades 3-6 who made all A's and B's for the third nine weeks (3 tablets, 2 Chromebook, and numerous other prizes, and will sponsor three parties this year for the first, second, and third semesters;*
- *Sponsored the Christmas party ($450) for our staff, since we had not had one during the two years I have been here;*
- *Sponsored Popcorn Fridays by purchasing a popcorn machine ($286) and all popcorn supplies for the entire year ($300);*
- *Sponsored my students' flights ($2,520) to Washington, D..C this summer;*
- *Anonymously paid two months' rents (December and January) for one of my students' parent who was facing eviction during the Christmas holidays;*
- *Purchased numerous supplies and clothes for students throughout the building who are in need.*

These are just some of the "giving" that I have done over the past two years, but I am absolutely sure none of these were discussed with you while concerns about me were being addressed.

With my credentials, I could teach anywhere I desire. I teach at Anna K. Davie Elementary because I truly care about these kids and sincerely want them to be successful. My grandmother was raised in a family similar to the kids I teach. She was the first in her family to graduate from high school. As a result, she and my grandfather, who only had a seventh-grade education, made sure all ten of their children received college educations (5 teachers, 2 nurses, and 3 dentists). I am living proof it only takes one spark to get a fire going. My goal is to be that spark these kids need.

Soon, I began to realize that Dr. Nicholson would never be able to focus on his job or the kids with me in his building. These sharks wanted blood and were not going to stop until they were able to eat me alive. I was content to answer concerns for the entire year if I needed to, but when my students started being placed in the mix, I knew it was time for me to resign.

One of my students was due to return from a suspension. Charles, *our new so-called behavior specialist*, had backed him into a corner. Evidently, he had threatened the student with suspension if he walked out of the room. Of course, the student walked right out of the room which never would have happened if I had been in the room. I was highly upset because I wouldn't have handled the situation in that manner. I always talked to the students privately and walked them through a conflict slowly to diffuse the situation. I made it known to Louise when she suspended my student that I didn't appreciate him being sent home, especially since the situation could have been deescalated. Furthermore, it was no secret that I handled my own discipline.

When I didn't see the student, I called the parent to see where her child was. She said, "He's at school!"

I asked the kids had they seen him, and they replied, "No."

I asked Charles to watch the kids while I walked to the front office to see what was going on. I didn't want to have a missing kid on my hands.

When I got to the front office, I was told the student was in Louise's office.

I went to her office, and he was just sitting there.

Louise claimed he was afraid to come to class. This was the same student who I couldn't get to go home in the afternoons. He lived in my class.

I said, "Okay, I will make sure he is taken care of."

This entire time, the student's mom was still on the phone. She was as confused as I was as to why her son was sitting in Louise's office. If he was in there as it was claimed because he was afraid, then why would I not be informed he was present but in the office. My student had been at the school for almost an hour.

The parent asked the student why he was in there, and he responded, "She was asking me questions about Dr. McCluskey."

The parent asked, "What questions?"

"She wanted to know if Dr. McCluskey is nice to us."

The mother asked him to give me back the phone and said, "I am on my way to the school. My child will not be used as a pawn against you." By the time the parent arrived at the school to speak to Dr. Nicholson about what occurred, Louise was no where to be found. At that point, even the students had figured out I had a target on my back.

20 RESIGNATION

By the end of August, I was at my breaking point. I was putting on a brave face for my colleagues, but the constant complaints had worn me down. I was reliving Cedartown all over again. Here again, it appeared as if another assistant principal was on a mission to destroy me.

My doctor had already increased my antidepressants to the highest dosage, but it seemed as if they had stopped working altogether. I was crying every evening on my way home and barely making it through the day without shedding a few tears. I was depressed and determined to get the depression under control. I went back to my doctor and was prescribed a second antidepressant to accompany the primary one. The combo probably would have worked, but the attacks increased. When I started losing my hair, I knew the job had to go. The job had become a detriment to my health.

I had been to the central office twice. Both times I met with the Patrick and Olive. They acted as if there wasn't anything they could do. They all but told me, "You can't prove any harassment is taking place against you!" But I knew it was, and so did many people around me. I refused to ask any of them to put their jobs on the line for me because I knew the school was not my major source of income, but it was for all of them. They would be crazy to stick their necks out for me when they could clearly see what I was going through. Who in their right mind would have wanted to change places with me.

When I went to work on August 25th, I was determined to be transferred, or I was going to resign. I hated to leave AKD, but I had to get away from the harassment. The day before, Louise contacted Dr. Nicholson while he was attending a conference, to tell him I harassed another teacher.

Dr. Nicholson texted me that afternoon and asked me, "What did you do today?" I had warned Dr. Nicholson earlier that the complaints were never going to stop, but he was an optimist.

I texted back, "Nothing…"

"Not what I've been told…smh" he texted back. His angry emoji didn't gel well with me. He didn't have a clue as to the amount of manipulation that was going on around him from those three individuals. Louise was bitter, and I could sympathize with her being bitter about the principal's job being stripped away from her. I only faulted her for not realizing that her anger should be directed towards Patrick and Olive, not me. I didn't make hiring decisions. During my two years prior, George never called me to his office about any complaints. Now complaints were being made almost daily, and some were beyond ridiculous.

Earlier that week, Dr. Nicholson had received a complaint from Louise that my students were unsupervised on the playground after lunch. She failed to mention that my students were being supervised by three second grade teachers. While half of my students were playing on the playground, the other half were with me inside the cafeteria. We were helping the custodians clean our cafeteria, because we were short one custodian. If I had known that this blatant lie was going to be told on me, I would have been on the playground instead of sweeping our cafeteria floor. The *Three Amigos* were simply taking advantage of the fact that Dr. Nicholson was new to the system and had no background knowledge of anything remotely related to AKD or my Facebook posts.

I rambled, "Let me see… I put a teacher of out my room! I'll have the PBIS up tomorrow! Check your email…I told Kay thank you for not bothering me! They never tell you the good! I did keep 14 kids who were not mine…missed my planning…shut down 3rd grade because the sub was about to walk out!!! But who noticed that…"

He never responded after that.

I warned Dr. Nicholson earlier that the complaints were never going to stop, and I was right. I told him the only way to deter the unfounded complaints and accusations was to require the individuals making them submit a written complaint, and allow me an opportunity to face my accusers. These people were determined to continue flinging falsehoods because they were hiding behind anonymity. If they faced me, they would have to tell the truth and show the proof, which they could not do. Unfortunately, Dr. Nicholson never did this. I recognized that he was pretty much in the same situation that Marvin, my superintendent from Cedartown, had been in years earlier. This is why I decided to ask for a transfer or resign.

I sat at my desk before my students arrived and drafted an email, which I sent to Patrick and Olive.

Olive,

May I please be transferred? If not…will December give you guys enough time to find a replacement for my class, and I'll resign.

My being at Anna K. Davie with Louise is affecting my health. As I explained to Patrick, it's not my fault that she was not selected for the principal's position. Her ire needs to be directed at you guys…not me. The environment that has been created towards me is becoming intolerable!

I will be more than happy to provide medical documentation since my antidepressants are now having to be increased!

v/r
Dr. McCluskey

Patrick's secretary called and asked me to come to the central office that afternoon to meet with Olive and him, which I did. I explained to the two of them once again that I felt I was being harassed by Louise.

Again, their stance was, "prove it!"

I asked them if I could please transfer.

Olive informed me that Patrick and she had looked at their personnel, and there were no available positions at the time *It wasn't until later on that I found out there was an open position at the middle school.*

I informed Patrick and Olive that since there were not any available positions for me to transfer into, I would resign. I asked for a sheet a paper and wrote my resignation letter as they watched:

August 25, 2017

Dear Rome City School Board:

I, Marilyn McCluskey, requested a transfer to another school in the Rome City School District due to continued harassment by my assistant principal, Louise. I have met with the supt. and assistant supt. on two separate occasions. At today's meeting, I was informed that there are absolutely no other positions for me in the Rome City School District, and that my offer to resign [effective] December 31st would be accepted;

although there are positions listed on our website.

I have served faithfully for two years. It is not fair that an employee has to experience harassment without any relief what so ever. Louise's ire should be directed toward Patrick and Olive for promising her a job for six weeks and then taking the offer back...not me!

I will miss the students and staff of Rome City, but remaining at AKD in the current environment is affecting my health. Effective December 31, 2017, I would like to resign from the Rome City School system due to harassment.

Respectfully,
Dr. Marilyn McCluskey

Dr. Nicholson was furious with me when I informed him I had resigned. He asked me why I had not come and talked to him first. I told him I refused to become a distraction for him, and before I became one, I would rather walk away. These kids needed him, and he would never be able to focus on them and improving the school as long as I was in the building. I hated to leave him alone because I knew that with me gone, he would probably be in the crosshair's next since there was far too much underhanded manipulation taking place in our building, all designed to make him fail.

Next, I texted Dr. Holland, the principal of the high school, that I had resigned. Like Dr. Nicholson, Dr. Holland and I also had a friend in common. My former principal, Mr. Hose, was Dr. Holland's fraternity brother, and the two of them had once been a member of the same chapter in Albany, Georgia. Mr. Hose had encouraged me to reach out to Dr. Holland about an assistant principal's position at the high school, but I never did. Dr. Holland and Mr. Hose were quite similar in that they both were very articulate, well educated, natural motivators, who made things happen.

Dr. Holland called me after receiving my text. Initially, I could barely talk to him because I was inconsolable. Dr. Holland's concern deeply touched me. He listened patiently while I blabbed on and on about how I had busted my behind for two years to better this school and the surrounding community, but the central office could care less. After I finished, he shared that he had also worked tirelessly and been passed over several times, but he didn't let it defeat him. He encouraged me not to give up because Dr. Nicholson needed me, and the kids did, too.

When I hung up with Dr. Holland, our conversation motivated me to send a rescission letter to the superintendent and board chairman, Faith. So I literally resigned and then rescinded that resignation about two hours later after receiving unexpected, encouraging words from Dr. Holland.

August 25, 2017

Rome City Board of Education
Rome City Schools

Rome, GA 30161

Dear Rome City Board of Education:

I wish to formally retract my resignation from Rome City Schools. Please accept this letter as retraction of my resignation letter dated today: August 25, 2017.

I look forward to continuing work with Rome City Schools. I apologize for any inconvenience this has caused.

Thank you for your understanding and consideration.

Yours sincerely,
Dr. McCluskey

By the time I hit send, a text from Dr. Holland had appeared on my phone. He texted: *Never let nothing or no one steal your passion. No struggle. No progression! We are built for this! Be strong!*

I was impressed; too bad he wasn't Rome City's superintendent.

THE AFTERMATH

After my resignation, I posted the following message on my personal Facebook page:

"We were buried therefore with him by baptism into death, in order that, just as Christ was raised from the dead by the glory of the Father, we too might walk in newness of life."

-Romans 6:4 (ESV)

The past three weeks have been trying for me at work. To say I can truly understand how Jesus felt when they crucified Him would be an understatement! I woke up this morning with His resurrection on my mind and realized that sometimes we have to resurrect circumstances in our own lives! This week, I'm stepping off the proverbial cross and hitting the reset button. I'm asking and praying for God to lift me up and enable me to "walk in the newness of life!" Life is too short for me to be stressed!
#risingagain #claimingavictory #Romans6:4#wont HEdoit! #depressionaintnojoke!

For the first time since the school year had started, I was at peace. It felt as if a huge burden had been lifted from my shoulders. The first thing I noticed was that the harassment stopped. The few coworkers who had kept their distance were speaking again. Everything was going so well that I thought Patrick and Olive had finally intervened. Things were beautiful again. Finally, we could now focus on improving our school.

Three weeks later, I still had not heard anything from the central office about whether my resignation or rescission had been accepted, so I assumed the latter must have been accepted. Still, there was no more drama directed toward me. Matter of fact, things were eerily quiet. Little did I know, it was once again, the calm before another storm.

Around 2:20 p.m. that Friday, September 15, 2017,

I received a phone call from Patrick's secretary, Mrs. Teresa Price. Mrs. Price is one of the nicest individuals I have ever met. Through all of my impromptu meetings and craziness spewing from the superintendent's office, she always treated me with dignity and respect. I always did the same and didn't hold anything against her because I knew she was only doing her job. I'm sure Mrs. Price could write a book of her own about the things she had seen take place around her, particularly since Patrick and Olive had arrived.

Mrs. Price asked me to come to the board's office to pick up a letter from the superintendent. I was on my way to Atlanta after work and asked if it was okay for me to pick it up on Monday. She told me that it had to be picked up that day. We went back and forth, and she finally told me the superintendent said to just report to his office first thing Monday morning. By this time, Dr. Nicholson had arrived at my room. I could tell by the look on his face he was distraught. I asked, "What is going on now?"

Apparently, Olive had just informed him that I was being reassigned to my house until December 31, 2017, because they were accepting my resignation and not my rescission. Wow! Now, I realized why the letter was so important. They were, in essence, paying me out of my contract. I had just made close to $35,000 for working only a little over a month. Did this system honestly need an ESPLOST [The Educational Special Purpose Local Option Sales Tax] after all?

I decided to get the letter that day, which also

happened to be Dr. Nicholson's birthday. Someone at the central office had a sick sense of humor. I didn't know how happy this birthday had been for him.

Dear Dr. McCluskey:

What is of the greatest concern to me are your continued statements in writing, in your resignation letter, in your request for a transfer the same day, and in other records from last year that you do not believe that you can effectively work at Anna K. Davie Elementary School. You have been unable to provide any basis for your allegations of "harassment," but I am nevertheless willing to agree to an assignment until December 31, 2017, whereby you will work from home and perform duties as may be assigned by your principal or by this office. This new assignment will be effective Monday, September 18, 2017.

Sincerely,
Patrick

After I picked up the letter, I took it to Faith, the board's chairman, to let her review the letter. I felt betrayed. Elaina, another member of the BOE who was a close friend of Charles, was at AKD that morning. I refused to believe either individual was aware of the decision that had been made concerning my employment. Was our system so dysfunctional that the superintendent could remove a teacher from the classroom without bothering to inform his board members? Exactly who supervised who, and where were the checks and balances?

They both swore they had known nothing about the decision to remove me from my classroom, rather than allow me to remain for the remainder of the year.

Granted, they may have been telling the truth. I just didn't believe them.

What baffled me, even more, was my recollection of meeting these same two ladies along with Charles and his wife at Starbucks in North Rome last school term around November. I met with them to inform them about the $300,000 21st Century after school grant. Being that I had worked with the program in Thomasville, I was familiar with it.

Initially Charles and I were going to apply for the grant through his nonprofit, but I had a change of heart and wanted to make sure the entire system was given the opportunity instead. I wanted to make sure that these ladies were aware of this grant opportunity. I had already emailed Patrick:

November 3, 2016

Patrick,

When is a good time for us to discuss the grant? I would like for you to present it to the board. Everything is a go on my end.

v/r
Marilyn.

Patrick responded twenty-five minutes later:

Good Morning Dr. McCluskey,

Is there a time today that would be good for you? I would like to bring Debbie with me to Anna K. Davie and all of us discuss the grant. What time would be good for you and we will come there? Any time prior to 2:30 PM would be good for me.

I met with Patrick and Debbie for over an hour explaining how the grant would benefit the system.

Debbie contacted me a week later asking me *if the DOE issued me an account username, password, etc. for the electronic platform when I submitted the intent form.* She informed me that she was putting together a grant writing team and would send information soon about the first meeting. I never received any information in regards to the meeting from Debbie and when the grant was awarded, I wasn't allowed to participate either. Louise selected the participants for AKD and purposely excluded me.

Imagine my surprise when Faith and Elaina informed me that Patrick had told the board about the grant, but they had no clue that it was me who had brought this opportunity to them. Patrick told them that the Title 1 director was the person instrumental in bringing this grant to his attention.

I was stunned. Why would Patrick and Debbie talk to me for an extended period of time, asking every question imaginable about a grant that they supposedly already knew about?

Whereas I was interested in discussing the grant, Faith and Elaina wanted me to know that they were interested in me possibly becoming an administrator in the system. They talked about the new school being built and their desire for more black administrators. I had been so wounded by Patrick and Debbie's betrayal in regards to the grant that I didn't even entertain their suggestion until Charles brought it up the following day.

I told him that me becoming an administrator in Rome City would never happen due to the fact I refused to be controlled. I remembered my experiences with being *given* a job in Thomasville and made it clear that I wasn't interested in any more favors from anyone.

I had realized for some time that these ladies' sentiment against me had shifted, but I had no clue that it had become bad enough for them to support me being gone from the system entirely. In all honesty, I had been warned by Elaina about my being so vocal about the disparities between the schools. When I started to reflect on the past year, it dawned on me that Charles was speaking with them more often without me. In the past, he would often call them in my presence; the phone would be on speaker, and I would also be apart of the conversation.

In the weeks prior to my resigning, on the few occasions that Charles conversed with either lady, he would leave the room and talk to them privately. Furthermore, on the day I was reassigned, Elaina had come to the school to pick up campaign shirts from another employee. Ironically, I had helped her find Charles during my planning period, because instead of being in my room, he told me that he was going to meet with students in the front office which he hadn't done before.

Now, I didn't think I felt crazy thinking that Elaina had tried to avoid me when she saw me the day I was dismissed. I knew Elaina and Charles talked that day privately, but Charles had not discussed the conversation like he normally did. Charles also didn't leave the school as normal on that day either which I did think was odd at the time. The proverbial cherry on top of all of the scoops of my paranoia was the fact that when I left AKD, numerous faculty and staff members reached out to offer support to me, everyone but Charles, the one who claimed to be my biggest supporter. Almost three months would pass before I heard a peep out him, and Faith and Elaina never returned my calls. I guess it is true what they say… *actions speak louder than words*.

Looking back on the day I was reassigned, Charles told me that he believed the decision to not let me remain for the remainder of the year was probably Olive's way of retaliating against me for requesting a list of candidates who had applied for her position. At the time, I thought his remarks were ludicrous. It wasn't until I received a copy of the applications I requested that I realized there might have been some validity to what he said. I may have rubbed her the wrong way after all.

After examining all of the applications, I was

stunned. Whereas all of the other applicants had completed the application in its entirety, the FOIA results showed Olive had not even bothered to fully complete hers. Absolutely no work history was listed on the application. I knew Patrick and Olive had worked together in a neighboring school system a few years back, which led me to believe that somebody may have gotten a hook up.

Whether or not Olive was given the position because of their acquaintance, I can't say with 100 percent certainty. However, I can attest to the fact that there were other applicants who appeared to have better credentials, including a current central office administrator who had also been a principal before and worked for the district for more than a decade.

It honestly looked bad to give an acquaintance, with an incomplete application, a job of that magnitude. To add insult to injury, this meant the Rome City Board of Education had unanimously voted for and approved an assistant superintendent with an incomplete application. I would think a job of this enormity would warrant board members reviewing the applications of the candidates for that position.

Furthermore, this situation would not have been so suspicious if the superintendent's wife was not head of the system's human resources department, a position that was formerly held by Dr. Dawn Kemp, a well-qualified, long time employee of the system. The same month that the superintendent was given his new position, he dissolved her job, which was chief of human resources and federal programs and reassigned her to the high school. Then, his wife became the system's human resources coordinator.

Dr. Kemp resigned.

Despite the fact that the public was told the wife would report to the chief executive officer, whose job the superintendent had spared, this was a textbook case of nepotism. What else could it be? Who rightfully dissolves the position of a human resources chief who has a doctorate and gives it to a person with an online bachelor's degree—a degree less than a year old?

Now I wondered if this was the reason Patrick had really dissolved the chief of human resources position. If my FOIA request hadn't been made to receive those applications, no one other than his wife would have been the wiser about the assistant superintendent's omissions. This was the perfect scenario for why nepotism is quite often considered troublesome.

At least Rome City pretended to go through the motions. Thomasville City's Board of Education voted to non-renew their high school principal's 2018-2019 contract and on the same day voted to hire his replacement. The replacement was hired without the job first being announced to the public. Only two board members, Dr. Hazel Jones and Dr. Mary Williams-Scruggs, voted against this decision.

If the Thomasville City community had not voiced their displeasure at the board for not following their own personnel policy to post all positions, those resigning/hiring decisions would have been business as usual. Kudos to the Thomasville community for holding their board of education accountable. Because of their protest, the Thomasville City Board of Education had to rescind the offer they made to the replacement principal and advertise the position, which is what they should have done in the first place. Either way, shame on both systems.

21 THE WORLD'S GREATEST PARENTS

Although my husband was born in Rome, Georgia, and has many relatives there, I am not from the area. I didn't realize how much of a family I had created in as little as two years. My students' parents were also upset with the announcement of my resignation. They didn't know about my daily struggles and how being at the school was affecting my health. I felt sorry for them because I knew things would possibly revert to normal for their kids after I left. Remember most of these were students who had practically lived in my principal's office because their teachers were kicking them out of class for a myriad of trivial reasons. I assured them that Dr. Nicholson would work with them in regards to any behavioral issues, and they needed to support him because he clearly did not have as much as I would have liked.

The parents supported my decision to rescind my resignation and informed me that they were going to address the board of education on my behalf. Their actions somewhat shocked me because it was rare for parents to speak up and support teachers when they are wronged, which is one of the major reasons most teachers remain silent. Teachers know that in most instances, they will not be supported.

Around ten parents submitted letters to Faith requesting they be allowed to address the board at their next meeting. She informed them that they would be addressing the board in their caucus rather than the official meeting. In other words, the chairman, a black female who is still the current BOE chairman, denied my parents their first amendment right to address the BOE publicly in an official capacity. I was flabbergasted when she informed us that it was *her* decision to restrict our speech.

There appeared to be a concentrated effort to ensure there was no formal record of the parent's concerns. To make matters worse, the parents were told they would have to address the BOE in the superintendent's office; it was too small to accommodate a large crowd. I was further surprised when Faith called the parents and told them they had to choose one spokesperson to speak on behalf of the entire group.

Never in my life had I witnessed anything of this

nature. I have addressed numerous boards during my teaching career. While many of these boards disagreed with me, not one had ever denied me the right to address them publicly during their meeting – until Rome City.

Despite all of the chairman's efforts to deter my parents from addressing the BOE, these parents were determined their voices would be heard. On the day of the meeting, almost fifty parents and students demonstrated outside the Rome City Board of Education prior to the meeting. Someone from the system called the police on the group in hopes of keeping everything out of the public view and behind closed doors like many of the other things they had done and gotten away with. There was only enough space for maybe ten people from the group to enter the superintendent's office.

The group's spokesperson, Ms. Tracy Smith, addressed the board on the group's behalf. She asked the board to accept my rescission and allow me to complete the year as their children's teacher. They knew I had decided I would no longer teach for Rome City after the year concluded. I had made it known to each of them that it was more important for me to try to open a charter school in Rome, Georgia, because the system had repeatedly failed to do justly for the black students at AKD, and it seemed as if they had no plans to change anytime soon.

I addressed the board and informed them my only regret was not addressing them about my being harassed before I initially submitted my resignation letter. The entire board had visited my room before (some on more than one occasion) and were well aware of the work I had done with the students, mainly my DLL students. Intelligent people should have easily realized there was more going on with my situation than they were possibly being told by Patrick and Olive. I wasn't surprised because I have found throughout my years in education that a lack of communication is a major issue many use to manipulate situations and intimidate others from speaking out when there is a wrong.

Typically, I do not share the deeds I perform for my students or their parents. These decisions are primarily between God and myself, because in Matthew 6:4 (NIV), we are told to give, "so that [our] giving may be in secret." It is for this reason that I prefer to keep my good deeds mostly private. Charles and I often fought over this because he always seemed to seek the spotlight and nearest newspaper. I am not about being seen, but rather doing what is best for kids. The parents in attendance were shocked when they heard all I had done for the school and their kids in the short period of time I had been there.

Despite my students' parents protesting and my speaking before the board and sharing all of my accomplishments since I had been with the system, the board voted unanimously that night to accept my resignation. It may have seemed as if Louise had won, and she had merely gotten what she wanted. But I was the real winner here. Now I could fully focus on writing the petition to get AKD students a charter school and write this book.

One of my students' parents called me later that night and said she had bumped into Elaina at Walmart. This parent was so excited because Elaina informed her the BOE had not voted on whether I could return or not. The parent was so enthusiastically hopeful I would be allowed to return that I couldn't help but tell her the truth. I told her Elaina had blatantly lied to her; the decision had been made that night and would be reported in the paper the next day. The reporter from the local paper had emailed me to let me know. I couldn't help but think if Elaina could so callously lie to this parent, exactly how many blatant lies had I been told over the past two years?

At that moment, I thanked God even more for the BOE's decision. Knowing my students would probably suffer this year, I found solace in the fact that they would soon have a charter school because I refused to give up until the State of Georgia approved our charter petition. Even better, I now had time to sit down and write a memoir of sorts about my time in public education and share with the world, in my own words, why I chose to walk away for good. Heck, if the book became a bestseller, I would be opening a school with my own funds until the petition was finally approved.

Six days after the parents' protest, Patrick asked me to come to his office to retrieve another letter. I figured we had ruffled some feathers and was expecting to be punished in some capacity. I opened the letter and read:

September 26, 2017

Dear Dr. McCluskey

This will serve as a letter of direction for your responsibilities, beginning immediately and for the remainder of your employment with Rome City Schools. I want to be as explicit and specific as possible in setting forth my expectations and the expectations of the school system as to your future responsibilities as an employee of this system.

School systems must be prepared to continue the education of students in the event of school closings. The development of an electronic lesson plan library is essential. Please utilize the Georgia Performance Standards to prepare three instructional days of lesson plans for each grade level in every content area (K-12). Determine the appropriate template but be sure to include all elements of an effective lesson plan. All lesson plans should be on this same template for consistency. Other tasks may be assigned.

Because you are still an employee of the Rome City School District, you are directed to be familiar with and abide by the Code of Ethics for Georgia Educators (505-6-.01): www.gapsc.com, and all policies set forth by the board, available on our website: www.rcs.rome.ga.us. Your workday is the same as for all teachers in Rome City Schools and is outlined in Board Policy GBRC (Professional Personnel Work Loads). You are expected to work a regular teacher schedule, and if you want to request leave or an absence, you will need to follow the guidelines outlined in Policy GBRH (Professional Personnel Leave and Absences).

You will be given a Chromebook to prepare the lesson plans. You are expected to either send the lesson plans that you have prepared by email to me each week or save them to a Google shared drive. Communication with Rome City School students and/or employees, other than the superintendent, assistant superintendent, or your principal during the school day is not acceptable.

*Sincerely,
Patrick*

After I read the letter, I laughed. I couldn't believe Patrick wanted me to complete lesson plans for an electronic lesson plan library. This was an utter waste of my time and totally retaliatory. It was no secret George exempted me from completing lesson plans. He and I knew it was impossible to create detailed lesson plans for fifteen different preps. I had followed curriculum maps instead.

I commented to Patrick, "Oh, I guess someone informed you how much I hate writing lesson plans."

He smiled and said, "No. We just need an electronic database for school closings."

I asked him exactly who was going to use these lesson plans. I explained that neither a parent or a student would need any lesson plans I would be writing. These plans had no lessons to accompany them, so they were useless for parents or students. Furthermore, teachers had emergency lesson plans that could be utilized in the event of a closure. It would make far better sense to allow me to create lessons that could be completed if the school was to close.

He wanted lesson plans.

I even offered to create Milestone study guides for AKD students and an accompanying mock milestone assessment to be administered.

He wanted lesson plans.

I couldn't believe the Rome City School System was going to pay me almost $35,000 for teaching a little over a month and writing lesson plans.

Again, is ESPLOST really a necessity?

22 OUTCAST

On election day, I promised my friend who was running for the Rome City Commission I would hold a sign for her that afternoon on Broad Street, the main street that runs through downtown Rome. On the way to hold her campaign sign, I stopped by AKD to talk with Dr. Nicholson. Now that my hormones had returned to normal, I'd recently remembered there was $600 in my New York trip account. After our trip to Washington, D.C., the prior summer, I had promised our students that our next trip would be to New York City. Since I would no longer be employed by the district, I wanted to discuss the possibility of taking the students to Six Flags during spring break with the money instead. I wanted to make sure they did go somewhere.

The kids and some of the staff were so excited to see

me that I felt like a movie star. Those who had been plotting for months to get me out of the building were in shock. I was only in the cafeteria for a brief time before Dr. Nicholson entered. When I noticed him, I asked if I could talk to him briefly about my intentions. I stated that I would not be able to stay long because I was on my way to hold up a campaign sign.

As soon as I entered his office, I excitedly stated how I had just promised Mrs. Freeman, one of the third grade teachers, and her class that I would host monthly level-up parties for them. I wanted to motivate these third graders to continue increasing their reading levels in the Reading A-Z program Mrs. Freeman was using in her class.

Before he could say a word, I advised him to create Lexile Clubs once again. This was a pet project I had been working on before my departure. Mr. Hose and I had created the 850 Club at MacIntyre Park for all kids who scored an 850 or higher on the CRCT, and it had worked phenomenally. I knew this same concept could help increase these students Lexile levels as well. I explained to Dr. Nicholson that to become a member of their respective Lexile Club, the student had to achieve the Lexile Level that the Milestone test deemed proficient. To remain in the club, the students had to maintain or increase their Lexiles. I offered to purchase Lexile Club dog tags for the students to wear around school.

Finally, I shared my idea about taking the kids to Six

Flags. Of course, he wanted to know who, how, why, and when? I educated him about the Six Flags Read to Succeed program. I thought this would be an awesome opportunity for AKD kids. Not only would the program motivate the kids to read more, but it would also enable us to earn FREE tickets to the theme park. Then the only expense we would have to cover would be transportation. I stated I had $600 sitting in an account that could cover the cost of the bus.

He wasn't familiar with the program but agreed it would be good for our kids. I told him we could kill two birds with one stone by participating. We would be motivating our students to read, and for many students, this would be their first trip ever to a theme park and for some, their first trip out of Rome, Georgia.

He shared that he had also been thinking about taking the students on a field trip to Atlanta. He wanted them to visit the King Center and Football Hall of Fame. I was pleased with either decision, but I was leaning more toward Six Flags! He was more than welcome to use the $600 to cover any transportation costs.

I had analyzed our CCRPI score from the previous year, which was a 55, and noticed our students' inability to read on grade level had hurt us significantly. I suggested to Dr. Nicholson that if our school could improve their Lexile Levels, then we could have a fighting chance at increasing our CCRPI score the current year. Our students thought they hated reading with a passion, but a mere two weeks before I was put out of my classroom, I showed them how fun reading could be. I also made each one of them read *Nightjohn*, the story of a slave girl who wanted to read so badly that she risked her life to learn. They were shocked when they read the scene where the slave who was teaching the little girl to read, had his toes chopped off as punishment.

I explained to my students that reading was so important during slavery, people were willing to kill and harm slaves if they were caught trying to read. I asked them what further proof they needed to realize how powerful it was to be able to read. I purchased almost $400 worth of books from Amazon, and they all had minorities as the main characters. The kids went bananas over the books. I knew the boys loved sports, so I had purchased them the *Amar'e Stoudemire Standing Tall and Talented (STAT)* series, *Tiki Barber's* series, all of the *EllRay Jakes'* series, and the *Carver Chronicles*. For my girls, I bought the *Keena Ford'* series, the *Sugar Plum Ballerinas'* series, *Ruby and the Booker Boys*, *Nikki and Deja*, *P.S. Be Eleven*, and *One Crazy Summer*. Finally, everyone in my class was reading because it interested them. They saw people who looked like them doing fun things they could relate to, and it made them want to read. I had originally bought these books so the kids would be able to participate in the Six Flags program.

I told Dr. Nicholson I had one more good idea to motivate the kids to read that I wanted to share with him before leaving; I had to go because I didn't want to be late getting downtown. I had shared this idea with George the year prior, but he had turned me down.

"I want to sponsor a limo for you."

His eyebrows raised, and he asked, "For what?"

I explained my idea to rent a limo to take the top students from third through sixth grades with the highest Lexile Levels and the students who had made the most growth from third through sixth grades to Applebees for lunch. A big grin plastered his face when I said this.

"C'mon, Doc, who doesn't like riding in a limo?"

We were about to discuss the details of the limo when his office door burst open, and the assistant superintendent walked in.

I looked in her direction and smiled. I was still excited about the potential limo ride and didn't pick up on her antagonist demeanor right away.

"Dr. McCluskey, I need you to leave the campus," she snapped.

This took me by surprise since I was not causing any confusion or commotion. Those kids who had seen me earlier in the cafeteria had been excited to see I was in the building. A few of them had snuck into Dr. Nicholson's office since it was adjacent to the cafeteria to say hi, but I had spoken to them and ushered them back into the cafeteria. Other than that, no one else even knew that I was in the building.

Olive pulled out her phone and said, "Do I need to read the letter that you were given?"

I replied, "The letter clearly stated I could meet with

Dr. Nicholson, and that is what I am doing." We were merely having a meeting, which was clear to any individual with a working set of eyeballs.

I had no plans to go anywhere else in the building because I was not stupid by any means. I was not taking any chances with the central office claiming I was being insubordinate. I had been there and played that game in Cedartown. I was by no means going to give RCS any reason to deny me any of my $35,000 - every last dime would be deposited into my bank account.

"Did you speak to any students or staff?" she asked.

I said, "It's lunchtime. Of course, I spoke to students and staff. Why wouldn't I during lunchtime?"

What was I supposed to have done? Looked at the individuals who had spoken to me and ignored them?

"I need you to leave now!"

The manner in which she spoke to me made me furious and reminded me immediately of how my assistant principal at Cedartown Middle would often address me when I worked there. I wanted to inform the assistant superintendent, as I had that assistant principal, that I was not her maid or her slave. But I didn't bother correcting her because I didn't want to star in the sequel to Cedartown. There would be no more scenes with the Georgia Professional Standards Commission (GAPSC) for me.

It was time for me to depart because I knew my being saved was only going to take me so far. I was still a work in progress.

Dr. Nicholson looked horrified. He was no longer sitting behind his desk. I guess he wasn't expecting two ladies with doctorates from the University of Georgia to be going back and forth in his office.

I slowly got up from my seat and walked to the door. Olive said, "I need for you to walk out of the front door."

Unfortunately, she was not going to get the pleasure of humiliating me in front of the front office staff, who were standing around with smirks on their faces.

I turned and walked out of the back door that led to the cafeteria. I could hear the assistant superintendent saying something in the background, but by this time, I had tuned her out. I was simply trying to focus on keeping my tears at bay long enough to get to my van. As soon as I entered the cafeteria, some of my students realized I was there and starting screaming, "Doc!"

They had not known I was in the building. I ignored their screams and walked even faster to my van. When I reached my van, I finally released the breath which I hadn't realized I was holding and starting bawling like a baby. I couldn't believe the assistant superintendent had embarrassed me like that in front of Dr. Nicholson, my former co-workers, and my students. It dawned on me, at that moment, that I was now an outcast. What right did we have to teach the students about bullying one another, when the central office leadership still had not gotten that memo? Furthermore, I had divorced the system, not my students or their parents.

I left the school and drove to the SunTrust Bank

down the street and sat there for a few minutes to compose myself. I didn't want my cousin who I'd be meeting soon to realize what had just happened to me. While I was ready to go home, I had promised my friend I would hold her campaign sign, and so that's where I headed.

As I prepared to get out of my van, I received a text from a coworker. I didn't know if she had seen the exchange or not, but from the message, I was fairly certain she was aware of what had happened to me. I read the text and almost started crying again. She sent a quote I had recently seen on Facebook:

> *When toxic people can no longer control you, they will try to control how others see you. The misinformation will feel unfair but stay above it, trusting that other people will eventually see the TRUTH, just like you did.*

As soon as I returned home, I drafted an email and sent it to the superintendent.

November 7, 2018

Patrick,

Am I banned from Anna K. Davie?

I was having a meeting with Dr. Nicholson, in his office, when Olive came over and asked me to leave the premises. According to her, I am not to have any contact with staff or students during the school day. I was not there to talk to any students or staff; I was there to talk to Dr. Nicholson and said hi to staff and students because it was lunch, which is when parents and mentors come; thus, I didn't see a problem saying hi.

I don't want any problems and would like to know if I am banned?

In January, when I am no longer employed, I will be eating lunch with several kids who I am still mentoring. It's embarrassing to be escorted out of the building, which I am sure was the intent!

Ironically, I was meeting with Dr. Nicholson to plan a field trip for the kids to the King Center and Football Hall of Fame in Atlanta. I have raised funds to sponsor the trip. I also offered to sponsor a level up party each month and purchase dog tags to help AKD's Lexile scores increase. These are ideas that helped me get huge increases.

In December, my relationship with the Rome City Board ends; however, my relationship with these teachers, students, and parents will be forever. I don't think it's fair to deny them extra resources to be spiteful toward me. It's not about me! We are all supposedly in education for these kids, and THEY should come first.

OAN: I have sent you several requests to address the board about our charter school. I am again asking to speak at the November 14th board meeting. At that time, I will also provide you an updated intent letter that reflects our name change.

Thanks,
Dr. McCluskey

As noted many times before, I was again denied the opportunity to address the board. As long as I worked for the system, I knew I couldn't fight this flagrant violation of my first amendment right. My contract was going to be over on December 31, 2017, and I promised myself the Rome City Board of Education would get their chance to meet the troublemaker in me.

Dr. Nicholson called me on his way home that evening. Before he could say a word, I said I was good, and there was no need for us to discuss what had occurred in his office. I warned him it might be best if he and I didn't have any more contact with each other. I didn't want his interacting with me to place a target on his back. Whether he agreed or not, I honestly don't know as I haven't spoken to him since.

DISAPPOINTED

2 Corinthians 11:13-14: For such people are false apostles, deceitful workers, masquerading as apostles of Christ. And no wonder, for Satan himself masquerades as an angel of light. It is not surprising, then, if his servants also masquerade as servants of righteousness. Their end will be what their actions deserve.

Still hurt by what occurred to me at AKD, I decided to write Patrick a letter to let him know how disappointed I was with him. I knew he had not been qualified for the job but had commended him before board members. I have always believed in giving people a chance, and sincerely believed at the time that he deserved one as well. Now I was beginning to realize why qualifications were so important. Unfortunately, incompetence produced chaos.

Had our superintendent ever been a teacher, assistant principal, principal, or even an assistant superintendent, he may have better understood what was occurring to me. I hadn't realized the extent that Patrick was not qualified to be our superintendent. He had not even taken the exceptional children's course, which is a basic level course that *all* educators in Georgia must pass prior to receiving a clear renewable teaching certificate. Our last superintendent ensured he remained in that position for two years and therefore qualified to receive a retirement salary based on the position. He literally left mid year after hitting the two-year mark.

It now dawned on me that Patrick may have only been interested in the position to ensure that he received his highest two years salary as a superintendent as well. Our teacher retirement is based on the most recent two years' salaries.

I drafted an email to the superintendent and poured out my heart:

November 8, 2017

Patrick,

I am sincerely disappointed in you. I can understand the politics of being a superintendent, but as a Christian and a pastor, I can't understand your persecution of me based on allegations that are not even true. No one has verified anything with me, and we all know where the manipulation is coming from and why.

I have always supported you. When you stood in my classroom, worried about whether the board would give you your job, I contacted board members on your behalf, as I promised. That's loyalty, which I have always been. In addition to that, you know what all I have done for the system. You and I both know that I brought you that $300,000 grant, and I told you when I gave it to you it would help your superintendence.

It's not even about my position anymore. It's about my reputation being tarnished by blatant lies you have not even afforded me an opportunity to address. You pretend to be outraged by my offensive Facebook posts, but I was telling the truth. Dr. Nicholson is being set up for failure, and Olive proved yesterday that he is indeed a "house slave by default." I wasn't embarrassed for me yesterday; I was embarrassed for him. Olive emasculated him in front of the entire front office, something I'm sure wouldn't have been done to George. I am certain that none of the other elementary principals would have been disrespected as Dr. Nicholson was yesterday, and none of their assistant principals would have blatantly gone over their heads.

I'm at fault for not wanting to partake of politics,

but that's only because my conscience will not let me sleep knowing how these black kids are not being educated in this system. The equity issue is glaring, and we all know this. I know my kids are going to be well educated. I'm a hypocrite if I don't want or expect that for my students as well.

If I have offended you, I apologize in advance. But I am sincerely hurt by your actions. I am also hurt by the recent attempts to paint me as an angry black woman, who is all of a sudden intimidating. Wow! I am a highly-educated black woman with three small kids and a teaching certificate. I would never jeopardize my family or my credentials for anyone, especially in response to the level of pettiness I have witnessed this past couple of weeks.

All I ask is that you pray about this situation as I have and sincerely do right by me. I'm at peace because I know that God has a purpose, and I wholeheartedly trust Him. It's He who touched my heart to reach out to you. I want peace between us.

God Bless You!

After my "disappointed" email, the superintendent sent me a response that stated:

November 8, 2017

Good Afternoon,

I wanted to let you know that I did receive this email and will respond to both items tomorrow.

Thanks,
Patrick

I was again summoned to the superintendent's office to pick up yet another letter.

November 10, 2017

Dear Dr. McCluskey:

On September 26, 2017, you received a letter of directive from me outlining your responsibilities for the remainder of your employment with Rome City Schools. In that letter, it states that communication with Rome City School students and/or employees, other than the superintendent, assistant superintendent, or your principal, during the school day is not acceptable.

It has come to my attention that you visited Anna K. Davie Elementary School on November 7, 2017, and that you were visiting students and teachers in the cafeteria. This caused a disruption in the cafeteria and is not acceptable as outlined in the letter from September 26, 2017. Therefore, I will be more explicit in my instructions that you are not to call, text, email, or in any way communicate directly or indirectly with the students or employees at any of the schools within Rome City Schools during the school/work day.
Your actions in visiting Anna K. Davie Elementary School on November 7, 2017, was in violation of the directive given to you in my September 26, 2017, letter and insubordinate. Please take notice

that any further insubordination or other incidents going forward could lead to disciplinary action to include termination.

Sincerely,
Patrick

As I suspected, Tweedle Dee and Tweedle Dum thought I was going to be stupid enough to give them cause to terminate my contract or an opportunity to send another insubordination complaint regarding me to the GAPSC. It was clear Northwest Georgia used the same playbook. I was so looking forward to December 31st. I couldn't wait to see what excuse they were going to come up with to keep me out of AKD. As a private citizen, I dared Patrick and Olive to violate my first amendment rights. There were now four new members on the Rome City Board of Education. I was hopeful that these individuals would not allow *business as usual* to continue in the system.

What amused me most about all of the foolishness that occurred during the latter part of 2017 was the happiness and relief I felt after my resignation. For those three weeks following my resignation, *The Three Amigos* had been eerily quiet. I was so ecstatic I was no longer being bothered, I informed Mrs. Perkins, the Performance Learning Center's administrator, who I had asked to pray for me, that things were finally perfect. I am tickled as I look back and reflect over those three weeks. It was another calm before another storm. It appeared I was no longer being harassed because the harassers had known they had finally succeeded.

Now I was going to sit back and let God and Karma do their jobs!

23 STEPPING OUT ON FAITH

"Sometimes God closes doors because it's time to move forward. He knows you won't move unless your circumstances force you. Trust the transition. God's got you!!!"
~Christine Caine

As I was looking for biblical Scriptures in regards to *moving on*, I came across the above quote. I don't know the author personally, but it resonated with me. Here I was wondering why God was allowing me to go through turmoil, (especially since I was living as close to righteous as possible, minus a few Sunday School words here and there) and the answer became vividly clear: God knew I was not moving forward in the direction He wanted me to go.

For over a year, I had been talking with my coworkers about us possibly starting a charter academy in Rome, Georgia since I was fed up with the politics running rampant in the system. I am not saying all systems are bad, but the bad ones are quickly outnumbering the good ones. The line between education and politics was becoming more and more blurred every day. Far too many individuals were focused on how they could achieve the highest salary possible for the two years needed to count toward their retirement. Others were dedicated to "hooking up" their friends to ensure their longevity in the systems. I'm okay with the occasional hook up; I would want to be surrounded by those I could trust. Being that education has become so cutthroat, I would definitely hire my *best and brightest* friends. While the adults are serving their own interests, the kids, particularly those of color, have become an afterthought as most systems could not care less if they are taught anything and only view these students as dollar signs.

Since my now "infamous" Facebook post supposedly led to AKD getting a black administrator, my talk of getting a charter had lessened somewhat. Ms. Roper would often ask, "Are you still going to get this charter thing going?"

I would assure her that we were still on track, but secretly, I was hoping the new principal would be the cure-all for our school, so much so that I didn't resign during the summer as planned. That's what tickled me most; I wasn't supposed to even be at AKD this school year.

Psalm 118:8 (NIV) tells us, "It is better to take refuge in the Lord than to trust in humans." I certainly should have followed the advice of this Psalm. At the end of my last school term when I informed my principal I had decided to remain home during the 2017-2018 school year to work on the charter full time, I should have stuck with that decision. I was delusional to think a new black principal could "cure" us. The powers to be were like the pharmaceutical companies who secretly prayed a new disease emerged so they could make more money pretending to look for a cure they genuinely don't want.

When I was reassigned to my home with pay, I felt a sense of relief since I had returned to education almost five years earlier. Most individuals would have been upset, distraught, or even embarrassed, but not me. I am amazed and overwhelmed at the power of God. God knew I needed to be forced out of my comfort zone to establish a charter school, so He pushed me out of the proverbial airplane. He knew there were numerous obligations to meet in order to establish a charter; obligations that are difficult to meet while teaching in a classroom full time.

Ironically, before I received my reassignment letter on September 18, 2017, I was trying to determine a time I could meet with three other charter school directors in Atlanta and Macon, Georgia. I still had the charter application on my desktop waiting for me to steal more time between creating lessons and grading papers to finally examine the document. Our consultant had just told me that a nonprofit had to be created because no individuals could hold the charter, only a nonprofit; the nonprofit research was still lying on my desk at home. I had planned to initiate the nonprofit process that weekend if I had a chance to possibly get started. There was so much that had to be done, but I had far too little time to do it. God made time for me!

My school system removed me from my classroom rather than let me rescind my resignation. Despite the protests of my parents, the school board unanimously voted no. In their defense, who knows what lies they may have been told about me by Louise, Olive, and/or Patrick. My uncle, Ulysses Marable, Jr., who was a board of education member for nearly 20 years in my hometown, told me years ago that the board members only knew what they were told. When it came to decision making, that information was the only source they had to rely on, so I wasn't mad at the board of education if they were duped. The thing that hurt me the most was the lack of communication. I believed I had established genuine relationships with some of the board members. For them to dismiss me without so much as a courtesy phone call stung to the core. I often corresponded with Elaina, and I knew that she was well aware of the retaliation taking place against me. I had shared many instances with her on several occasions. The least she could have done was made the other board members aware of what was truthfully going on.

I know being that "voice" can actually change a situation in which someone is being wronged. I have been that voice on many occasions. When I was in Valdosta, I convinced my principal to give my cousin, Elizabeth, a job. My cousin taught at our rival Valdosta Middle School, and her principal had non-renewed her after one of her students had brought a BB gun to school. The students eventually told on him, but my cousin was accused of not monitoring the class. Elizabeth was monitoring the class; the problem was she had been given two classes to monitor and was required to rotate between the two. When she made me aware of this situation, I shared what had occurred with my principal and made it known that Elizabeth was not the problem; their lack of adequate staffing was. I asked my principal if she would allow Elizabeth to come to Newbern. Not only was my cousin a hell of a teacher, she also had three small children that she was raising alone. She needed her job.

Even though Elizabeth had been told the system's policy was another principal could not hire any employee who had been non-renewed by their principal, I knew my principal could get around this since she was good friends with our superintendent.

Elizabeth and I were attending a science conference when my principal informed us that my cousin would be coming to our school. Not only has Elizabeth been named Teacher of the Year for Newbern Middle since this incident, she still works for Valdosta City to this day. If I had not spoken up for her, Valdosta City would have lost a phenomenal employee who has touched the lives of many teachers and students.

Ironically, that same principal also wanted to non-renew my teammate, Pamela. My principal felt my teammate didn't need to be at Newbern since she so-called couldn't handle the students. It wasn't that she purportedly couldn't handle our students per se; I thought Pamela was more suited for an elementary setting. Additionally, because she was white, many of our students would try to take advantage of her kind nature. While she wasn't the only white teacher at Newbern, she was one of three on our eighth grade hall which had twelve teachers. My experiences, as the only black teacher in Cedartown, made me hyper vigilant. I made sure that the minorities (whites) around me were supported.

For instance, my coworkers threw me a fabulous baby shower for my son, Derrick, my first year at Newbern. I noticed during the shower that my other teammate, Karen, looked a little sad. I knew that was not her nature, so I asked her what was wrong.

"No one threw me a shower last year," she informed me.

My heart sank. I was sure it was probably an oversight, because as I said earlier, the ladies on the eighth grade hall were like family. As I suspected

Karen's baby was born during the summer, and no one had thought to throw the shower during the fall. Needless to say, Karen became pregnant a short time after my shower. I was determined that she would have not one shower, but two (since we technically owed her one). The kids and I threw her a shower, so I would have an excuse as to why my classroom was decorated for the surprise shower that was to take place after school. The teachers and staff threw her a fantabulous shower after school. I remembered her mentioning that her dad was a dentist in Alabama after she found out that my family was full of dentists. I asked her off-handed questions about his practice until I obtained enough information to contact her family. I invited Karen's family to the baby shower. Her mother was tickled pink and was excited to participate. Karen's family drove all the way from Alabama to Valdosta to celebrate with us.

Pamela was friends with another principal who had agreed to allow her transfer to his school, but if my principal did not renew her, she would not be able to transfer. When Pamela informed me of the situation, I went straight to my principal and asked why wouldn't she allow Pamela to transfer. My principal told me that she didn't think this individual needed to be a teacher. I explained to her that my Pamela was a great teacher. Her lessons were well thought out and taught to our students, and she cared tremendously for them. I'll be the first to admit, Pamela may not have been a strong disciplinarian, which is not uncommon for many people who work in inner-city schools, but she cared about our kids.

"Furthermore, she is not transferring to teach. She is transferring to become a media specialist," I informed my principal.

My principal replied, "Tell her to bring the transfer paper today; she only has today, and I will sign her transfer," which she did. My teammate transferred to her new school, where she didn't have any problems and remained in the system almost another ten years until she retired last year.

Both of these individuals would not have been in the system, and the students would not have benefited greatly from their presence if I had not spoken up. I have always been a voice of reason to those around me in education. In a group, there must always be a voice of reason to ensure decisions are made to benefit stakeholders. Everything that God has made is filled with goodness. I'm going to always look for that shred of goodness, despite the evil or wrong which seems to surround it.

This year wasn't the first time lies had been told on me, and I was sure it would not be the last time that I was the victim of false accusations. I am grateful to the Rome City Board of Education for being the straw that broke the camel's back for me. If they had allowed me to remain until the end of the year, I wouldn't have worked as hard as I am now to open a charter school. I would still be at AKD, comfortable, content, miserable, and frustrated with the lack of progress.

To many, my current situation may have seemed bad, but for me, it was a sign from God. I get goose bumps every time I think about how He not only has gotten my attention, He has pretty much pushed me in the direction that He wants me to go. I no longer have to find time in the midst of my hectic schedule to work on tasks that needed to be done to work toward establishing a charter school. Since my departure, I have more than enough time. God has also led me to the people who possess the knowledge to help us make our charter become a reality. The CEO, Mr. Ehab Jaleel, and principal, Ms. Cherisse Campbell, of Amana Academy in Fulton County, allowed me to visit their charter school during their Stemventure Day. Amana is the number one K-8 STEM Certified School in Fulton County. These two awesome individuals have introduced me to expeditionary learning and other individuals who could assist us with our charter process. Every time I have found myself facing obstacles with the charter, God has guided me in the direction needed to overcome any hurdles.

Stepping out on faith required me to leave my comfort zone and totally trust God. With my credentials, I could have easily obtained another job teaching somewhere else, but I chose to step out on faith instead. I stepped out on faith and finally said goodbye to public education after nineteen years. I said goodbye to all the times I had been called "pro-black" because I demanded better curriculum, programming and services for students of color. I said goodbye to all the times I was retaliated against for simply telling the truth. I said goodbye to all the times I had been unjustly stereotyped as being the angry black female. I said goodbye to all of the times administrators had tried to stifle my creativity and place me in a box. I said goodbye to all of the coworkers who didn't believe that all children could learn regardless of how they looked or where they were from. I finally said goodbye to the overall tomfoolery that permeates the public education system!

EPILOGUE

He replied, "Because you have so little faith. Truly I tell you, if you have faith as small as a mustard seed, you can say to this mountain, 'Move from here to there,' and it will move. Nothing will be impossible for you."
~Matthew 17:20 (NIV)

Since I have finally completed my book, I am now devoting all of my time to opening a charter school, which I initially was going to call Rome City Charter Academy. After everything that has transpired with the Rome City School System, I absolutely no longer wanted a name that remotely resembles theirs. I called Ms. Roper and asked, "What would be a worthy name for the charter academy? I want something biblical because I sincerely believe God has a purpose for this school and me."

She and I tossed some names back and forth, and she finally said, "What about Cornerstone Charter Academy?"

I loved it, and from there, Cornerstone Charter Academy was birthed. The charter petition process is a fairly complicated one, but I am confident the founding board and I will complete the petition when we get to that part of this process. If our petition is approved, our academy will open for the 2020-2021 school year. I wanted to rush this process and try to open a year earlier, but I have come to realize that God does things on His time and not mine. In order to be as successful as possible, our charter school must establish partnerships, which takes time.

We have become members of the Georgia Charter Schools Association (GCSA) and enrolled in their Incubator Program. GCSA was created in 2001 and is a membership organization for Georgia's charter school operators and petitioners. We are confident that with their assistance, our dream to open a charter school will come to fruition.

What has shocked me the most is how ignorant many people are about charter schools. Charters are quite often confused with private schools, and the two are different. Charter schools are public schools which means they receive public funding and cannot charge any tuition. They must also have fair and open enrollment. In other words, anyone can attend a charter school. Charter schools must also be nonspiritual and are required to serve all student populations, including students with disabilities and English language learners (ELL).

The main difference between a charter school and a traditional public school is autonomy and flexibility. Charter schools are usually governed by a non-profit board of directors, instead of a local board of education; and they receive flexibility from certain state rules and regulations in exchange for a higher level of accountability. It's this flexibility that charters use to implement innovative and unique programs that aren't offered in traditional public schools.

The one complaint that I keep hearing repeatedly is that our charter will take money from the public school systems in the area. Here is reality. Charter schools not approved by the local board of education do take funding away from local systems, but those approved by local boards do not. It would be a win/win for the local board to work alongside us, but it's difficult to do when Patrick, the superintendent, has told me that "charter is a dirty word" and refuses to allow me to address the Rome City Board of Education about your willingness to work with them. That is the only reason that we are seeking to become a state-chartered school whereby our charter will be authorized by the State Board of Education only.

Unfortunately, because we will be chartered by the state, we won't be able to receive any local funding which is ridiculous since our students will also have parents who pay property and state taxes. Why shouldn't their kids also be allowed to benefit from their hard earned dollars? Being a state charter will also make the local system lose funding since a certain amount of funds will follow the students who choose to enroll in our charter. Who knows, maybe a board member will read my book and finally discover the truth.

To be brutally honest, the opposition has been shocking to say the least. The police chief, the executive director of the Northwest Georgia Housing Authority, and the executive director of the Rome-Floyd County commission on Children and Youth, all declined to partner with us. With a third of Floyd County kids living in poverty, a local rate higher than state and national averages, I would think that these ladies would have been willing to partner with us to help educate the youth of Rome. Our founding body is made up of a group of teachers who are tired of politics as usual and simply want to educate children. We understand that education can improve the lives of these kids. All we want is an opportunity, free of politics, to prove it.

Our goal is to ensure that Cornerstone is a premier charter academy that focuses on educating the entire family. We will offer our students a stellar STEAM (science, technology, engineering, arts, and math) learning experience and will include Spanish courses from K-8. Instead of participating in only two activity courses (music and P.E.) as currently offered to the majority of Rome City Schools' elementary students, Cornerstone plans to offer technology, art, music, robotics, and Spanish to all students. Additionally, we plan to offer GED courses on site for our parents, host monthly parental developmental courses, and operate a parent resource center geared toward helping our parents become self-sufficient. Our focus is on bettering the entire family so that our students' lives can improve socially, emotionally, and financially. What better way to help our students than by strengthening their families?

I finally visited Anna K. Davie again in February. One of my students asked me to come eat lunch with her for her birthday. At first, I was reluctant to go back to the school. After the fiasco with Olive, I didn't want any more problems. Unbelievably, Dr. Nicholson, Olive, and Patrick were all gone to visit a charter school in Atlanta.

Won't HE do it?

I was able to eat lunch with my student without any incidences. I had prayed for God to move some mountains for me, and it appeared He was listening loud and clear; however, a new visitation policy was adopted after my visit. Now visitors must be escorted to the lunchroom and no one can supposedly visit classrooms any longer. After this book's release, I am sure the school's attorney will come up with some creative way to have me banned from all Rome City School properties altogether!

People truly do fail to realize that I divorced Rome City Schools. I didn't divorce my Anna K. Davie babies. Many of our students and their parents have become an extended family to me; thus, RCS needs to realize that we have "joint" custody, because I am not going anywhere anytime soon. I plan to continue fighting to make things better for Anna K. Davie students. All of my book sales from Rome, Georgia will be donated to Anna K. Davie to purchase playground equipment for the students. We are still the only school in the system without a decent playground. Our kids have one climbing toy to play with at this time. Although Berry College has a smaller playground for their 3 year old classes, our students are excluded from playing there…and it still has only a smaller climbing toy. There are no swings, merry go rounds, slides, etc. I'm determined to get Anna K. Davie students a decent playground since it doesn't seem the system will be getting them one anytime soon.

Lastly, I did finally get a chance to talk with Dr. Nicholson. I encouraged him to not give up on our school. I feel his year was basically sabotaged, but it seems as if those who were doing most of the mischief have decided to leave.

That *move mountains* prayer is something else.

Now Dr. Nicholson has an opportunity to build a supportive staff, so next year should be a much better one for our students and him.

Speaking of moving mountains, Olive resigned. Is it possible that God has a sense of humor? Ironically, Olive will be working from home on a special assignment.

Sounds familiar?

I will never savor another's misfortunes, so I will keep her uplifted in prayer. She may not see it now, but

God has a bigger blessing on the horizon for her as well. Ironically, if she had only given me a chance, she and I could have made a heck of a team. Her views about educating children from low socioeconomic backgrounds are very similar to mine.

ABOUT THE AUTHOR

Dr. Marilyn Mitchell-McCluskey was raised in Dixie, Georgia. She is a nineteen-year veteran educator, a profession she entered after deciding not to become an OB/GYN. After the birth of her oldest son, she realized she also had the gift to teach like her mother, a former educator with 34 years of experience. *Stepping Out on Faith* is her first published work. Soon, she will publish her second book, *Lesson Plans*, which is a labor of love she has been working on for several years.

Dr. McCluskey is the daughter of Thomas/Linda Gosier and Marion/Velvie Mitchell. She has seven siblings: Glen, Johnny, Angela, Thomas, Allison, Anthony, and a twin brother, Marion. A mother of four children: Marion, McKenzie, Blanche, and Derrick, Jr.; Dr. McCluskey is married to her Fort Valley State College sweetheart, MAJ (Ret) Derrick William McCluskey.